The Impact of Trade Destruction on National Incomes

A Study of Europe 1924–1938

PHILIP FRIEDMAN

A University of Florida Book

The University Presses of Florida
Gainesville

Library of Congress Cataloging in Publication Data

Friedman, Philip   1945–
    The impact of trade destruction on national incomes;
a study of Europe, 1924–1938.

    (University of Florida social sciences monographs,
no. 52)
    Bibliography: p.
    1. Europe—Commercial policy—History. 2. Europe
—Commerce—Mathematical models. 3. Income—Europe
—History. I. Title. II. Series: Florida.
University, Gainesville. University of Florida
monographs. Social sciences, no. 52.
HF1531.F74   339.2'094   74–6172
ISBN 0–8130–0450–0

Acknowledgments

THE ORIGINAL idea for this work was the result of research pursued in Professor Charles P. Kindleberger's course on European Economic History, at the Massachusetts Institute of Technology.

Professor Peter Temin (M.I.T.) was supportive at every stage of the work, providing encouragement and insightful comments. Professors Edwin Kuh and Jagdish Bhagwati (M.I.T.) served as readers, and their comments were helpful and illuminating. The work as it appears here is a revision of my doctoral dissertation at M.I.T.

I consider myself very fortunate to have studied economics at M.I.T. A general acknowledgment of an intellectual debt to, and the kindness of, colleagues and faculty is tendered.

Mrs. Marjorie Friedman kindly consented to provide editorial assistance.

I finally acknowledge an incalculable debt. My wife, Marilyn Sue Friedman, provided the necessary ingredients of inspiration, perseverance, and love which enabled me to complete this work.

William E. Carter

For

EUGENE FRIEDMAN
1905–1971

Manual Laborer, Historian,
and Father

Contents

Is there anything that a tariff could do, which an earthquake could not do better?

JOHN MAYNARD KEYNES

If one country has good harbours while all the rest have bad ones, it will not realise the advantages of its good harbours so fully as if all the rest had good ones also. But it will realise some advantage; it will be better off than if it, too, sank rocks all round its coast.

ARTHUR CECIL PIGOU

1

Goals, Methodology, and Specific Applications

THE HISTORY of European commercial policy is replete with cases of aggressive and restrictive policies. The interwar period provides the best example of the use of restrictions by states which are experiencing the effects of an economic crisis. These states turned to restriction in an effort to secure protection from the contraction around them. All of the policies employed had the effect of restricting trade, whether indirectly through the market or directly via governmental controls. One aim of this study is to measure the extent of trade destruction resulting from commercial policy. There are welfare effects of restrictive commercial policies which adversely affect income via trade. An additional goal is the quantification of the implied, measured, and estimated losses of national income.

The major question, therefore, is the impact of trade restriction upon national income. There are two parts to the answer. I quantify first the proportion of income loss caused by reduced trade, and second, the share of this loss caused by the set of restrictive policies pursued during the depression. The second stage necessitates an investigation of the model to be used for the quantification of the policy and trade effects. Behavioral questions (which are dealt with in the form of hypotheses tests) arise which concern the constancy of tastes for imports (a question about the constancy of import propensities) and the significance of subgroups of nations in explaining differential propensities and policies.

Since the trade destruction observed is coincidental with a host of commercial policies, and the assumption that commercial policy and trade are connected is highly reasonable, I must quantify the commercial policy changes in order to investigate the trade-induced income losses. This does not imply an assumption that the total trade change was the result of policy activity. Therefore, an explicit test of the policy and trade interaction is conducted. Policy effects

1

on trade are crucial in a model where policy enters as the link among crisis, trade, and income. The model which emerges is one in which commercial policy drives the system of prices and trade, which in turn determine income.

Ideally, the analysis should be based upon a general equilibrium model of traded goods, capital flows, prices, income, and commercial policies involving all of the nations of the world and all of the international flows among all nations. I did not proceed in this manner for two reasons. The first is purely prosaic: the information necessary for such a modeling does not exist. The second is philosophic: even in the absence of data problems, I am not convinced that there exists a specification which would adequately capture the essence of the system and events of Europe between the world wars. Given the nonquantifiability of some of the more important events of this period, and the absence of a viable world model, the feasibility of such a project is questionable. In light of these problems, I turn to a second best but feasible approach. There exist sufficient data for an estimable econometric study covering a subset of European countries. The econometrics would not include intercountry flows and, therefore, would lack explicit simultaneity. However, there do exist intercountry trade flows for all nations for separate time periods. There is also a vast qualitative history of the period. By performing three separate but interrelated studies and using as many of the results obtained as input into the model, perhaps an insight into the events of the period can be provided.

It is fruitful to consider the research as three separate but related passes over the same data and period. Since there is no single approach which can capture adequately the essence of these international trade and income effects, perhaps the combination of a historical survey, an analysis of trade flows, and an econometric model can provide an adequate understanding and measurement of trade destruction and national incomes.

It is arbitrary which point in time one chooses to begin a historical investigation. While there are obvious watershed dates and events, no event stands isolated from the past. Data restrictions may be helpful in choosing that point in time, but if they were the only criteria, economic history would be bounded by the shortest continuous series, and this is not the case.

The history of European trade is the history of commercial policy, most of which is restrictive. Since this first section is an attempt to deal with the historical aspects of restrictions, I must begin sometime before the period under observation. Data and relevance combine to limit my initial date to just after World War I, with some occasional references to earlier dates. The remainder of the period is divided into subperiods comprised of initial depression, post-depression, and recovery phases. The classifications are the result of economic events which will be dealt with during the discussion. The history will attempt to illuminate trends in the commercial policies of various nations. Policy trends and events will form the basis for the construction of commercial policy series, which will be used in the estimation of a formal model. Moreover, it is hoped that the investigation will aid in the determination of the initiating causes and lines of interaction among national policies.

The time span of the remaining sections is determined by severe data restrictions, which include the absence of national income data and the incompleteness of other data for all but a few nations prior to 1924. Since 1924 is the first date in which reasonable post–World War I recovery occurred, and is also when the hyperinflations of central Europe ended, it appears that the constraint of that date as the beginning of the study period is not exceedingly restrictive. The latter date, 1938, is chosen as the closest date to World War II when data are accurately reported and not yet severely affected by mobilization.

The trade flow data between the wars are only available for three dates: 1928, 1935, and 1938.[1] The restriction placed upon the research by the number of dates of intercountry flows is mild for some aspects of the study and severe for others. The data provide enough time differentiation for investigation of the behavior of trade levels and trade balances over the period. All of the countries considered attempted to improve their own balances of trade. However, since this was accomplished at a lower level of overall trade, there were adverse effects upon income generated by these countries' policies. The determination of the effects of restrictions upon the flow of trade is only partly successful, due to the scarcity of data points. While the flows provide enough information to enable us to measure the extent of some restrictions (generally bilateralism), they are too gross for the investigation of the effects of tariff policy changes. A few questions concerning changes in the direction of trade flows

1. League (43), (44).

as a result of policy actions are posed, but the answers are inconclusive.

The trade flow data provide enough information to enable determination of the major lines of trade interconnection. This information is necessary, since the lines of interconnection among countries will point to the proper specification of a model of trade and policy interaction.

Last, by looking at contemporaneous trade and income levels, the flow data can provide gross estimates of the income loss from trade. These gross measures will be the first appraisal of the trade and income relationships. The measurement of these relationships will be refined by the estimation of an appropriate model.

The final section is the specification and estimation of an econometric model of income, prices, trade, and commercial policy during the period under study. The model will be a trade-dominating Keynesian macro-model.

There is extensive literature on the estimation of import propensities in Europe during the thirties, most of it simplistic.[2] The major postwar work is by Neisser and Modigliani (30). Polak's study (32) provides the initial ground rules and Neisser and Modigliani provide the starting point for the construction of the model. I begin with a simple linear Keynesian model in which foreign trade multipliers are generated, using import functions. These import functions are estimated at first with only an intercept shift reflecting the possibility of changes across the depression. This model is tested and compared to alternatives which have a more flexible set of assumptions about the changeability of coefficients. These sets of single regression equations provide some insight into the movement of import propensities. The equations, however, fail to capture several crucial elements of the trade process under investigation: they lack quantified commercial policy variables; they include the assumption of income exogeneity which is untenable; and the basic interaction of other country commercial policy and income levels on import functions is omitted. Consequently, these equations cannot be used to generate estimates of income losses under alternative assumptions which would be used to infer the size of income destruction due to policy and behavioral activities. These qualifications led to the development of a simultaneous model with "own country" policy as

2. Cheng (10), a complete survey through 1960.

exogenous and "other country" policy, plus "other country" income and world data as instruments. This specification allows the use of information from the historical and trade flow sections to be used as input into the estimating procedure. This input takes the form of variables used directly in estimation and in the choice of instruments.

The estimation procedures used are ordinary least squares (OLSQ) and two-stage least squares with instrumental variables (TSLQ). In estimation, both regression types are combined with scanning techniques for correcting autocorrelation. In addition, a specialized large regression technique is employed to test propositions about groups of equations.

The coefficients generated by these processes are, in turn, used to generate multipliers. These multipliers, which are qualified by tariff level and tariff revenue retention assumptions, are used to estimate the effects of commercial policy and trade upon income. The estimates are also used to reach policy implications based upon the impact of commercial policy changes. Policy implications are also garnered from comparisons of generated income values, which are implied by the model under various policy and taste assumptions, with income values using actual policy conditions. These generated income levels are also used to answer some questions about disaggregate behavior.

The data restrictions on income and price narrowed the field of available countries in Europe from more than twenty to twelve.[3] This group of twelve is a set of countries which did in fact typify the economy of Europe.

In summary I attempt to generalize from the diverse sets of estimated values, and to put the policy information into sharper perspective by discussing overall trends in policy and trade.

3. Belgium, Czechoslovakia, France, Germany, Netherlands, Sweden, Switzerland, Bulgaria, Denmark, Finland, Hungary, United Kingdom.

2

A History of Commerical Policy in Twentieth-Century Europe

In order to assess the degrees of change in postwar policy conditions, some mention of the prewar policy state is necessary. Since the repeal of the Corn Laws,[1] the United Kingdom had followed an unwavering policy of free trade. Only a small number of articles were subject to duty of any kind, and the duty levels of these remained unchanged until the first decade of the twentieth century. In 1910, the first tariff changes occurred, in the form of increased rates upon certain foodstuffs, beverages, and consumer products. These were the only new rates until massive protection began during the war.

The Netherlands was the only continental nation which followed England upon a course of free trade. Her free trade policy was unchanged until the start of World War I, when the first duties, of moderate value, were imposed.[2]

Germany, having previously initiated rather severe protection, adopted a moderate protectionist policy at the turn of the century. The level of these moderate duties was to remain stable until the outbreak of war.[3]

France had a long history of protective policies. In 1910, she initiated an upward revision of the existing rates and raised the ceiling on maximum rates which could be administered.[4]

In 1906, Switzerland, in response to the general trend of rising duties, raised its rates on foodstuffs and manufactured goods imports. These rates also continued without change until the beginning of the war.[5]

1. Barnes (2).
2. Isaacs (18), p. 360.
3. Ashley (1), pp. 60–109.
4. Ibid., pp. 269–355.
5. Isaacs (18), p. 359.

The years 1903, 1906, and 1908 saw the upward revision of tariff rates in other European countries. These rates stabilized, along with French and German rates, until the war.

The prewar state of commercial policy was dominated by two trends: the constancy of British free trade and the ten- to twenty-year stability of moderate continental protection. These trends were severely altered by the war.

The proliferation of types and levels of trade restrictions employed during World War I was enormous. Almost every European nation resorted to restrictions, either in the form of tariff changes, surtaxes on existing duties, quotas, licensing restrictions, or complete prohibition of foreign trade.

The question of protection versus free trade in British social and political life is a complex topic concerning conflicting interests and conflicting groups. The long history of free trade was probably the result of self-interest rather than ideology. The country was not eternally wedded to free trade but, rather, embraced the concept when conditions for such an alliance were favorable, and abandoned free trade when faced with the financial and political crises produced by World War I. In 1915, Britain introduced the McKenna duties, and in 1919, imperial preference was strengthened. Both policies laid the foundations for a new protectionism.[6]

Before the war, France had the highest and the most complicated tariff structure in western Europe. The war produced two changes in French policy. First, tariff rates and coverages were increased. In 1918, rate minimums were raised from 5 to 20 per cent, and maximums were raised from 10 to 40 per cent. Over four hundred items were on the revised duty lists, including almost all manufactured goods. The second change concerned the type of restriction. The use of licenses and coefficient systems enabled an ad hoc changeability to dominate commercial policy. In 1916, special associations of merchandisers and manufacturers were granted exclusive licenses to trade in certain classes of imports. In 1919, licensing arrangements were widespread. Moreover, an innovation in administered rate increases was employed. A system of coefficients was designed which would multiply the level of any existing tariff without changing or revising the current tariff law.[7] The importance of the coefficient system, which was determined by an interministerial commission,

6. Benham (3), p. 25.
7. Isaacs (18), p. 369.

lay in the formalization of an ad hoc procedure. During this period the coefficient sizes ranged from 1.1 to 3, i.e., a 10 to 200 per cent increase in rates. French administrators could subsequently alter tariff rates at will without entering into a legislative process, a fact which becomes more important in the later years of the period.

Germany imposed complete trade prohibition during the war. Her commercial policy immediately following the conflict will be discussed separately, in considering the causes for changed postwar policies.

The Netherlands, issuing no changes in policy during the war, remained a bulwark of free trade.[8] Belgium, Italy, Czechoslovakia, Turkey, and Poland had major tariff revisions during and immediately after the war.[9]

POSTWAR COMMERCIAL POLICIES

While it is obvious that wartime considerations increased levels of restrictions, why did Europe not return to prewar policy levels once hostilities ceased? The general answer is that postwar Europe was essentially different, in many crucial aspects, from prewar Europe. The differences, in terms of implications for policy, can be seen in a set of postwar conditions which made a return to prewar policies impossible.

Protectionism.—The very fact that protection was initiated or increased during the conflict was a reason for its continuance afterward. Protection creates vested interests: protected sectors can only survive with continued protection.[10] This ratchet effect, in terms of policy, was most evident in Britain. In 1921, the United Kingdom passed the Safeguarding of Industries Act, which included a set of protective tariffs covering manufactured goods deemed either to have special importance for the security of the nation during time of war or to be of outstanding importance to industry. The latter consideration was coupled with a doctrine of comparative cost. If the import price of any good covered by the act was below an arbitrarily determined minimum profit price for that domestic industry, then a tariff of 33⅓ per cent was applied. Just after the war, the criteria for which industries were to be included under the act were

8. Ibid., p. 374.
9. Chalmers (8), p. 12.
10. Beveridge (4).

obviously more closely related to protection than to national security. The industries chosen included coal, iron, steel, engineering, ship-building, electrical trades, textiles, chemicals, and a number of other minor industries.[11] In the same year there occurred the passage of two other articles of legislation which were unique in their rejection of the principles of free trade. These policy acts reinforced the notion of vested interest in continuing protection. The Dyestuffs Importation Act prohibited, except under license, the importation of all synthetic dyestuffs and intermediate products. Commercial policy for the protection of a single industry had not been employed since the Corn Laws. The Reparations Recovery Act set a precedent of discrimination against trading nations. It set rates of up to 50 per cent against German imports only.[12] While this legislation was in direct contradiction of British support for most-favored-nations (MFN) clauses,[13] its passage was legalized by the nonreciprocal MFN stipulations of the Versailles Treaty. This was only one of many discriminatory constraints placed upon German trade and the German economy, some of which will be discussed in consideration of other causes for changes in postwar policies.

Despite the restrictions upon her commercial policy, Germany in 1922 was still able to raise tariff rates on manufactured goods by a small amount, and in 1923 by a substantial amount (50 to 100 per cent). In addition, she invoked a licensing system on trade and manufactured goods. This was an attempt to exert further control over trade policy, in spite of the conditions of the treaty. The absence of duties on foodstuffs was the result of severe shortages in staple commodities rather than a loosening of policy attitudes.

Hyperinflation.—Another postwar condition which made the loosening of restrictions difficult was the state of domestic currencies. During the early 1920s, many continental countries suffered severe inflation. The condition reached hyperinflation levels in central and eastern Europe, especially in Germany and among her former allies, Austria and the newly created states. Hyperinflation and massive devaluation are part of the same phenomenon. Restrictive policies undertaken by European nations in reaction to the devaluations contributed to continued protectionism after the war. The extent of devaluation varied considerably in Europe. The percentage of the

11. Benham (3), pp. 29–30.
12. Ibid., p. 31.
13. Snyder (33).

value of the dollar relative to the par value for national currencies is used as a measure of devaluation. This rate never exceeded 120 per cent for the countries with stable currencies. These countries included the United Kingdom, Netherlands, Sweden, Switzerland, and Norway. Nor did it exceed 500 to 700 per cent for the moderately stable currencies of Belgium, Finland, France, or Italy. The rates of devaluation are of a much larger magnitude for the currencies of high inflation countries, ranging from 1,500 to 8,000 per cent in Bulgaria, Greece, Portugal, Roumania, Czechoslovakia, Yugoslavia, and Estonia. The devaluation rates for currencies in hyperinflated Germany, Austria, Hungary, and Poland all exceeded 1,000,000 per cent.[14] Such major changes in relative currency prices would have, without a response, caused equally large changes in trade balances. The reaction of almost all of the countries in the first two groups (those with stable and moderately stable currencies) was the placement of restrictions upon the exports of the second two groups (high inflation and hyperinflation currencies), especially upon the exports of the last group.

In 1922, England imposed a 33⅓ per cent duty on all imports emanating from devalued currency countries.

France had abolished the coefficient system by 1920. In its place she had levied prohibitive tariffs on a large percentage of previous imports, essentially upon all nonnecessities. In the face of massive devaluation, what was once a specific tariff of prohibitory size becomes equal to an ad valorem tariff with a miniscule rate. France revived the coefficient system and applied increasing coefficients to the imports of devalued currency countries. By 1922, over 3,000 tariff rate changes involved coefficient alterations.[15] Even large increases in tariff rates were insufficient in prohibiting imports. France turned to direct control of trade via quotas. This first use of quotas, based on a 1910 law, would act as a precedent for France's commercial policies in the latter half of the interwar period.

Debt structure.—The postwar structure of intercountry debt contributed to the continuance of restrictive commercial policies after the war. The financial cost of World War I left most of eastern Europe in debt through loans and/or reparations. Without getting embroiled in the transfer controversy, it appears that there was still a huge incentive for these countries to pursue policies which would

14. League (41).
15. Isaacs (18), pp. 369–70.

generate export surpluses; among these policies was the restriction of imports. However, they were not in a position to simultaneously lower imports, pay reparations, and support the minimal demands of their populations for consumer goods. Credit flows of capital were required to maintain the gross importation of goods necessary for survival as long as these nations attempted to stimulate their export markets. Even with the critical state of domestic supply, some trade restriction was practiced. The degree of restriction would have been much greater in the absence of loans from western nations.

Political structure.—Two final postwar conditions which contributed to the inertia surrounding protective policies were the result of the changed political character of postwar Europe. This political restructuring led to economic dislocation across national borders (the placing of previously internal economic processes into the arena of international trade), and to nationalism arising from the creation of new states. Furthermore, this new nationalism affected these states' commercial policies. Not only were borders changed because of the creation of new states, but victorious nations were granted portions of their defeated neighbors, mostly at the expense of Germany and Austria.

The new nations were faced with serious questions of viability. Europe, before the war, had an established system of specialization and trade. Keynes wrote, in *The Economic Consequences of the Peace*, "The interference of frontiers and of tariffs was reduced to a minimum, and not far short of three hundred millions of people lived within the three Empires of Russia, Germany and Austria-Hungary. The various currencies, which were all maintained in relation to gold and to one another, facilitated the easy flow of capital and of trade to an extent the full value of which we only realize now when we are deprived of its advantages."[16] The reality of prewar Europe was not as rosy as Keynes portrayed it. Yet, he is correct about Europe's interdependence which developed in spite of moderate but reasonably stable restrictions, especially regarding the trade between Europe and Germany.

> The statistics of the economic interdependence of Germany and her neighbors are overwhelming. Germany was the best customer of Russia, Norway, Holland, Belgium, Switzerland, Italy, and Austria-Hungary; she was the second best customer of Great Britain, Sweden, Denmark; and the third best cus-

16. (23), p. 15.

tomer of France. She was the largest source of supply to Russia, Norway, Sweden, Denmark, Holland, Switzerland, Italy, Austria-Hungary, Roumania, and Bulgaria; and the second largest source of supply to Great Britain, Belgium, and France.

In our own case we sent more export to Germany than any other country in the world except India, and we bought more from her than any other country in the world except the United States.

There was no European country except those west of Germany which did not do more than a quarter of their total trade with her; and in the case of Russia, Austria-Hungary, and Holland the proportion was far greater.[17]

Prewar Germany supplied manufactured goods to a highly agrarian central and eastern Europe. Austrian financial centers were supported by intracountry trade within the empire. Had the dissolution and creation of states been accompanied by a strict adherence to free trade, there would have been no economic consequences since intra- and international trade would not have been differentiated except by name. Free trade was not to prevail. The new states now had the ability to pursue policy goals which either were not voiced, or were voiced and not acted upon, by the old political units of which they were only regions. This nationalism led to the construction of chauvinistic commercial policies designed to encourage a growth in industrialization via export markets. The result was, of course, a less efficient system of goods production. It would be impossible to infer that a welfare loss resulted from the loss in production, since it was possible that there were changes in tastes in favor of home country output.

The transfer of raw material resources from Germany to France and Czechoslovakia (Alsace-Lorraine and Upper Silesia) involved the movement of an input flow from an intranational, nonrestricted context into an international trade context with all of the restrictions mentioned.[18] It is obvious that the Versailles Treaty was not written with the purpose of maximizing any pan-European objective function, economic or otherwise. What was maximized were the conditions for disruption of the prewar European production process. New states were following nationalistic goals toward industrial autarchy, which, though never attained, exhibited a certain movement

17. Ibid., p. 17.
18. Ibid., p. 85.

toward self-sufficiency. The older states used realigned borders and restrictions to change Germany's economic position.

Between the turn of the century and the end of World War I, there was considerable change in positions of comparative advantage, both inside Europe and between Europe and the rest of the world. This was especially true of agricultural production. Western hemisphere grain producers were posing a competitive threat to European agriculture. Had market prices been allowed to generate resource reallocation, there would have been no severe disequilibrium. However, the war had afforded protection, which, once implemented, is difficult to remove because of the tenacity with which the protected attempt to retain their favored position. This was true of many producers in Europe, especially in agriculture, because of an additional political force behind their protection. In Germany and France (and in most of the rest of the continent), agricultural producers represented a political class which the postwar governments had a stake in protecting. This political protectionism was over and above any economic gains or losses the governments may have thought were associated with the policy. In general, the reluctance of the postwar European countries to undergo the readjustment and reallocation which the changed conditions necessitated contributed to an environment where restrictionist trade policy was encouraged.[19]

In addition to the stated restriction, the war and its aftermath brought about the advent of administrative ad hoc trade restrictions, which included both direct governmental action (confiscation and arbitrary rate changes) and bureaucratic obstruction (needlessly complicated customs regulations). This trend toward qualitative restriction was to return in force during the latter part of the interwar period.[20] The basis for this type of policy was founded in the reaction to postwar conditions.

Though there was some movement toward relaxing the extreme level of international trade restriction after the war, the conditions allowed only a slowing down (if anything) in the spread of regulation.

To summarize, World War I had left Europe with a grim legacy. Part of that legacy was a number of conditions under which a return to free and unrestricted trade was almost impossible. Vested interests

19. League (47), 1:30–35.
20. Condliffe (12), Introduction.

formed by wartime protection, plus hyperinflation, the postwar structure of debt, economic dislocation across national borders, nationalism and the formation of new states, and ad hoc administrative controls, combined with a resistance to readjustment and reallocation, all formed the bases for continued restriction.

Despite these conditions, the postwar European economy began to grow. The need and desire for a movement away from the restrictionist trend was evident. There were even some signs of a slow but visible improvement in trade relations as Europe began to emerge from the legacy left from the war.

MOVEMENTS TO IMPROVE TRADE RELATIONSHIPS

Between 1924 and 1925, Europe started a slow but definite recovery. Not only were some of the aforementioned conditions ameliorated to some degree, but the economies of most countries improved almost to prewar levels.

The major improvements (in postwar conditions) which had an effect upon the relaxation of restrictions were currency stabilization, resettlement of the intercountry debt structure, and the advent of commercial reciprocity. The first two of these were closely related.

Currency stabilization was absolutely necessary. It was achieved in Poland by 1924, in Germany and Austria by 1925, and in Hungary by 1926. This stabilization was only possible with the aid of United States capital flows and a resettlement and reconstruction of the intercountry debt structure. The reforms incorporated in the Dawes Plan were crucial for the monetary reformation of eastern Europe.

Economic nationalism began to give way to some forms of international cooperation. The new states began to discuss negotiations for commercial reciprocity. These agreements culminated in the Danubian Confederation settlements of 1927.[21]

In spite of the reformation in currency, debt, and reciprocity, there was still considerable inertia regarding restrictionist policies. In the aggregate, this is evidenced by a comparison of European and rest-of-the-world production and trade movements.

By 1925, production levels outside Europe had reached approximately 125 per cent of their 1913 levels. In Europe, the same production measures equaled their 1913 levels for the first time

21. Chalmers (8), p. 30.

(102 per cent). A quantum measure of non-European trade was between 124 and 140 per cent of 1913 levels, while the same measure for Europe was only 90 per cent of the prewar level. Trade, growing faster than production in the rest of the world, was lagging behind production in Europe. Though there are no good income data comparable to prewar levels, contemporary reports indicated that the European economy, except for trade, had returned to 1913 levels.[22]

In a later chapter, a formal model of trade and income will be discussed. However, at this point the simple relationship between increased income and increased demand for imports would imply that restriction should have begun to decline. This is especially true in the face of the removal of some of the conditions encouraging restriction. The restrictions did in fact recede, but not by very much.

Between 1924 and 1926, all of these countries had tariff revisions: Austria, Belgium, Bulgaria, Cyprus, Denmark, Estonia, Finland, France, Germany, Greece, Hungary, Iceland, Ireland, Italy, Lithuania, Netherlands, Norway, Poland, Portugal, Roumania, United Kingdom, and Yugoslavia. On average, this group of revisions was not clearly upward or downward. However, they were all consolidations of previous law and, in most cases, replacements for administrative controls. Licenses were also replaced by tariff measures throughout the continent. Between 1925 and 1926, Germany, Hungary, Austria, and Czechoslovakia abolished their licensing bureaucracies.[23] To the extent that known tariffs replaced uncertain administrative and bureaucratic control, trade restrictions were lowered.

Germany was under external constraints regarding the pursuit of its commercial policy because of conditions required by the Versailles Treaty. On January 10, 1925, the five-year requirement that Germany offer nonreciprocal MFN treatment came to an end. The rest of Europe was faced with these choices: to continue anti-German trade discrimination and face an almost certain retaliation, or to end the discrimination and sign commercial treaties with Germany. Even though Germany followed a more restrictionist tariff policy during the period, the threatened retaliatory war did not materialize. Germany signed MFN treaties with Italy, United Kingdom, Netherlands, Switzerland, Austria, Hungary, and Turkey, and

22. League (47), pp. 83–108.
23. Chalmers (8), pp. 23–38.

limited or transitional treaties with Belgium, Spain, USSR, and France.[24] Franco-German trade relationships reflected the two countries' former roles as victor and vanquished. France was the most tenacious European country in terms of her desire to retain some form of anti-German restriction. Her tenacity weakened in 1927 with the signing of a commercial treaty, which included provisions for full mutual MFN status by 1928.

Until 1927, France's commercial policy was dominated by the coefficient system, which had become the most cumbersome, restrictive, and protective system in Europe. Between 1927 and 1928, the levels of the coefficients were raised twice, each time by approximately 30 per cent. This rise in coefficient levels brought the effective tariff rates up to and above the rates employed during both wartime and postwar devaluation crises. It was during this time that France replaced the coefficient system with commercial treaties. In addition to the treaty with Germany, France signed over fifty other treaties, fixing tariff rates and abolishing the further use of coefficients. The major European treaties were with Italy, Switzerland, and Belgium.[25]

There was no appreciable change in policy after 1927–28 (except for minor downward revision) for any continental country until the crisis of the Great Depression.

The United Kingdom, having embarked upon a postwar path of protection, reversed its policy in 1923. The general election of that year was interpreted as a rejection of protectionist policies. The McKenna duties and the duties of the Safeguarding of Industry Act were allowed to lapse. Relaxing restriction even further, the U.K. reduced duties on sugar, tea, and other staples. The movement was, however, short lived. A Board of Trade inquiry in 1923 established that a group of goods was suffering from the effects of "unfair competition and/or dumping." The Conservative party argued for the imposition of tariffs on those goods, but was vigorously opposed by the Liberal and Labor parties. A Conservative victory in 1924 led to a series of tariff revisions between 1925 and 1928. In 1925, tariffs of 33⅓ per cent were placed on whole classes of processed textiles, household utensils, and some paper goods. In 1926, tariffs of 16.7 per cent were introduced on paper products, petroleum products, and small manufactured articles. Between 1927 and 1928 25 per cent tariffs were placed on ceramic and metal household

24. Ibid., pp. 27–38.
25. Woytinsky (34), p. 270.

goods, photographic goods, tobacco, and wine. In 1929, duties on iron and steel were nearly enacted when a Labor victory changed governmental policies. This victory was supposed to generate large-scale removal of duties, but only a small number of downward revisions were actually undertaken before the depression crisis of the thirties.[26]

Most of Europe continued protection and restriction after the war. Although recovery brought with it some slowing down of the increases in rates, there was no visible movement toward a rate reduction. In the latter part of this period many proposals for duty increases were defeated. Whether this is the result of a loosening of policy restrictions, the observation of proposals for bargaining purposes, and/or some international cooperation is impossible to determine. However, it was evident that there were formal structures where cooperation in trade was advocated.

There were a host of international conferences, many of which were sponsored by the League of Nations. The conferences conducted during this period were intended to deal, either exclusively or in part, with international efforts to secure the removal of prohibitions and restrictions. Recommendations of the Supreme Economic Council and the Brussels Financial Conference (1920), the Portorose Conference and the International Chamber of Commerce Conference (1921), and the Genoa Conference (1922) all argued strongly for both a removal of the highly restrictive postwar policies and a multinational cooperation toward free trade.

The first set of recommendations was concerned with the removal of obstacles to trade created by excessive, arbitrary, or unjust customs formalities, fraudulent trade practices, single state discrimination, administrative or legal measures, nonpublication of tariff regulations, unnecessarily obtuse nomenclature, and even more trivial and esoteric restrictions. These recommendations were essentially endorsed by all of the participating members of each conference. Furthermore, the conference members were able to record reasonable success in translating the recommendations into policy changes in their home countries. The second group of recommendations was both more general and less effective in that they were less acceptable to all delegates and less able to be translated into policy action at home. These policy principles had as goals a restoration and improvement of the freedom of commerce that existed before the war,

26. Benham (3), p. 31; Liepmann (28), pp. 131–33.

the abolition of prohibitions and quantitative restrictions on trade, the stabilization and reduction of tariff rates, and the conclusion of long-term commercial treaties incorporating full MFN conditions. Of these, the last was the most successfully fulfilled.[27]

Between 1924 and 1927, several small conferences and committees tried, in vain, to improve upon the work of the meetings in the early twenties. The World Economic Conference of May 1927 was the most successful of these efforts to bring about international agreements to end restrictions, but the actual changes in policy were not as striking as the formal declarations submitted at the conference.[28] Twenty-nine countries, including the United Kingdom, France, and Germany, adopted an international convention stating, in part, that within a period of six months, they would abolish all import or export prohibitions or restrictions and not impose any thereafter, the only exception being the adoption of prohibitions and restrictions which were, in extraordinary and abnormal circumstances, vital to the interests of the country. Obviously, the exception clause, interpreted on an individual basis, was the undoing of the resolution. In spite of this loophole, the Economic Consultative Committee of the League of Nations filed a report in May 1928 concerning the effect of World Economic Conference conventions. It concluded that "The Conference has already substantially checked the upward movement of tariffs which was in full swing in May 1927. . . . Proposed increases in certain tariffs (France and Norway) in preparation in May, 1927 have been moderated; reductions in duties, generalised through the MFN clause had been effected as a result of several bilateral treaties and in a few countries by autonomous action (Czechoslovakia); elsewhere insistent demands for increased protection has been refused (Denmark and Netherlands)."[29] The observed policy changes were hardly the same as those presented in the convention, and in the light of increased duties in France and Germany, the conference failed in lowering restrictions while it may have been successful in preventing further increases.

By 1929, there was no appreciable change in policies, nor was there any indication as to the future course of European commercial policy. While no clear trend emerged other than a slow continuance of postwar restrictions, the question was academic. By

27. League (38), pp. 15–29.
28. Ibid., pp. 32–51.
29. Ibid., p. 43.

1929–30, the effects of the beginning of the depression were being felt throughout Europe, and commercial policy and trade were not to be exempted.

THE EARLY PHASES OF THE DEPRESSION

While an attempt will be made to isolate the effect of policy and trade changes on income during the depression, the extent to which the prior conditions of deteriorated postwar trade contributed to, or caused, the depression cannot be measured here. I can assert, however, that those conditions were part of an overall set of political and economic circumstances which contributed to the depression. The exact prime and remote causes, their timing and interactions, are still the topic of serious debate which will not be laid to rest here. However, I will consider the set of depression impacts upon the European economies as exogenous. While this may violate a strict interpretation of exogeneity, in a historical context it can be reasonably argued that commercial policy reacted to the exogenous shocks delivered by the depression.

The shocks were heterogeneous and, for our purposes, qualitative. These outside changes included a change in capital flows, the advent of an international monetary crisis, the collapse of agricultural prices, a decline in British trade demand, and a move toward increased restriction in U.S. tariff policy.

A sudden change in capital flows, which among other things was sustaining eastern European imports, has been pointed to as a candidate for the initiation of the depression. The flows slowed down and finally disappeared during the early course of the depression, and an argument can be made for their effects upon commercial policy. As a result of the change in flows, intra-European imports fell while the need for foreign exchange to meet debt obligations rose. Both of these changes may have resulted in a more aggressive trade policy.

An immediate result of the international monetary crisis was devaluation. Devaluation in one country had the effect of lowering the degree of protection afforded by previous restrictions in other countries. In reaction to the dilution of their restrictions, affected countries retaliated via their own devaluation and/or more restrictive commercial policies.

The effect of a rapid fall in world agricultural prices was to increase greatly the propensity toward agricultural protection which had developed in postwar Europe, especially in France and Germany.

The other two shocks to the European trade system surely would have been considered endogenous in a world model of policy, trade, and income. These actions can be viewed as exogenous from the standpoint of the continent. The first of these was the income decline of the United Kingdom. The continental demand for U.K. exports represented a smaller portion of total British exports than the U.K. demand for continental Europe's exports, the latter of which represented a considerable share of European foreign trade.[30] In addition, the large-scale interaction of the British economy with the rest of the world (mostly the Commonwealth) indicates the degree to which U.K. income can be viewed as being free from continental influence.

The second shock was the change in U.S. tariff policy in 1930. The Hawley-Smoot tariff is traditionally credited with having a huge impact upon European commercial policy.[31] This tariff, more a reaction to U.S. internal conditions than a reflection of external trade policies, could have affected Europe only in one or more distinct ways. The impact in Europe must have operated via a significant real export loss, or through a neighborhood effect resulting from the abrogation of international treaties, or through some expectational mechanism. Europe's trade with the U.S. represented between 5 and 7 per cent of total European exports.[32] These were relatively small compared to intra-European percentage rates for 1928: Europe, 64.8; France, 63.7; Germany, 71.9; industrial continental Europe (ICE), 70.9; and nonindustrial continental Europe (NICE), 85.7. While U.S.-European trade did fall off considerably, the losses were much less than inside Europe.

It cannot be concluded that the impact of the Hawley-Smoot tariff in Europe was the result of an initial abrogation of agreements which had been made restricting countries from changing tariff rates. As seen earlier, France, Germany, and the U.K. had already violated those agreements.

The Hawley-Smoot tariff was a drastic change in policy for the U.S. It not only represented for Europe the prospect of decreased

30. 14 vs. 23 per cent, respectively, for western Europe in 1928.
31. Jones (22).
32. For 1928: U.K., 6.3; France, 5.8; Germany, 6.6; nonindustrial continental Europe, 4.9.

trade with America, but perhaps it was also an indication of America's unwillingness to support Europe in the future. The implications of this for capital markets, future commercial treaties, and the general trend of commercial policy probably operated through some unspecifiable expectations mechanism. The U.S. tariff may not have been an identifiable shock, but combined with other circumstances, Europe may have reacted to it, though not in any clearly identifiable or strong manner.

Britain's commercial policies can be seen as having a greater measurable effect upon the rest of Europe than any of these events. Through several policy actions, the U.K. would create very visible disruptions by her reaction to the depression.

POLICY DURING THE DEPRESSION

Though conventional wisdom places the beginning of the Great Depression on a Black Friday in October 1929, a European viewpoint of commercial policy may reasonably place the onset of a major crisis between 1930 and 1931.[33] This conclusion is based upon observations of the changes in policy, income, price, and production variables.[34] It is necessary to focus on the reaction of trade and commercial policy to the depression, regardless of arguments which attempt to place the indirect causes of these reactions in the late twenties or even at the end of the war. Therefore, the relevant data are the timing and intensities of exogenous variables during the depression when policy and taste behavior changed. The strongest candidates among the choices of relevant exogenous actions which elicited a policy response on the continent were the changes in British commercial policy.

Britain's policies.—Of the major policy changes undertaken by Britain—the flight from sterling, increased protection, and heightened imperial preference—the first was most clearly related to economic events in the rest of Europe. All of the policies were, in part, a response to the culmination of a growing crisis, and all were interrelated to some degree. This fact casts doubt on their independence. However, it is hoped that considering the policies as separate outside shocks and tracing the reaction to them is valid. Even a partial

33. The exact date depends upon which European country is being considered.
34. League (47).

acceptance of this caveat requires some discussion of the events leading up to the flight from sterling.

Banking panics (national or international) reflect rapid reactions and exploding expectations. The panic that first surfaced in Austria and proceeded to England was of this type. The Macmillan report and subsequent May report detailed the extent to which British short-term assets and £150-million gold reserve were considerably below short-term liabilities.[35] In addition, a large proportion of the short-term assets were in the form of loans to eastern Europe. When the European financial crises surfaced in May 1931 with the fall of the Austrian Creditanstalt, a banking panic was underway. While this was not the "start" of the depression, the extent of the crisis and the commercial policy reaction to it point to this event as a turning point in the deepening and intensifying of the depression. In a national panic, the crisis is precipitated when, for any reason, depositors in general wish to convert bank liabilities into some other asset. The fractional structure of the banking system makes such a general conversion impossible. In the face of this impossibility, each individual inability to convert reinforces depositors' desires to convert.

Even a partial conversion can only be accomplished by a fully loaned system with the infusion of high-powered or outside money. An analogous situation developed internationally. The run on Austrian banks and, later, on German banks represented a desire to convert internationally, i.e., to shed domestic currency and demand deposits. The high powered/outside money would have had to have been foreign exchange or gold. Britain was caught in the cross fire. Previous short claims on Germany were now frozen. This further reduced England's short position. Smaller central banks of Belgium, Netherlands, Sweden, and Switzerland began selling off sterling reserves to meet specie and other currency demands. During the last week of July 1931, the Bank of England lost over £25 million in gold. The bank secured a £130-million loan from France and the United States, but by mid-September credits and reserves were exhausted. On September 21, 1931, the Gold Suspension Act was passed. Sterling was allowed to float freely and it immediately depreciated, by 20 per cent in September and 30 per cent in December. Denmark, Finland, Sweden, Norway, Portugal, and a large

---

35. Benham (3), p. 12.

portion of the Commonwealth abandoned gold before the end of September.[36]

If the sterling crisis can be viewed as an aggravated balance of payments problem, then the solution would lie with either devaluation or tariff policy (the Macmillan report suggested a tariff). The abandonment of gold immediately solved most of the problem. In a technical sense, there was no problem from the British point of view. Sterling, now floating on world markets, would move to the market price which would balance payments.[37] Viewing the floating of sterling as a de facto devaluation which had an effect on continental commercial policy requires us to investigate the effectiveness of the suspension on continental trade. If the British policy was to have had no other effect than a simple-minded devaluation response from the continent, we could leave the matter there. Conversely, if British devaluation affected continental policy by causing the continent to react by protecting itself from a change in its import demand for British goods, we then have to establish a terms-of-trade effect resulting from British suspension.

Taking the suspension to be a de facto devaluation ranging between 20 and 30 per cent, the effect on terms of trade is determined by the size of relative elasticities. The condition that the sum of the import and export elasticities of a trading partner exceed unity in order for the terms of trade to improve for the devaluing country (Marshall-Lerner condition) can be reasonably demonstrated as holding for Britain vis-à-vis continental European countries during this time period. Neisser and Modigliani (30) have estimated manufacturing elasticities for England. Their import elasticities range from 1.17 to 1.63, and their export elasticities range from 1.01 to 1.27. My overall British import elasticity is 0.815. Therefore, the overall export elasticity would have had to have been less than 0.185 to violate the Marshall-Lerner condition. Britain's nonmanufacturing export elasticity would have had to have been extremely low, and nonmanufacturing exports would have had to have been a sizable portion of exports in order to bring the export elasticity of approximately 1.13 down to below 0.2 overall. That the nonmanufacturing elasticities were sufficiently low is improbable. Furthermore, it is untrue that the nonmanufacturing sector of exports was a sizable portion of the total. In addition, the reasonably sizable

36. League (47), 1:77–82.
37. Benham (3), p. 24.

percentage of British exports into Europe,[38] combined with the overall import elasticities of 0.52 and 0.23 for France and Germany, respectively, argue for acceptance of the fact that the Marshall-Lerner conditions were satisfied. Therefore, in the absence of retaliatory devaluation, there was an export-stimulating effect for British goods.

While the sterling countries did devalue, the gold bloc nations of France, Switzerland, Netherlands, Italy, and Belgium did not. These countries suffered a change in their terms of trade. The ˙non–gold bloc, nonsterling countries suffered the same change without retaliation. As would have been expected, both groups of countries did, in fact, retaliate—against the British suspension and against the coincidental change in British tariff rates.

During the crisis in the fall of 1931, a general election took place in England. The election ushered in the conservative national government. A substantial number of its members favored protection, especially as a reaction to the ongoing crisis. It is not clear whether the new government viewed a change in tariff policy and/or suspension of sterling as independent and individually sufficient policies from Britain's point of view. Also, it is not known whether or not the government was able to, or wanted to, separate the protection of domestic industry via tariffs from the use of tariffs as a short-run remedy in crisis.

Within three days of the election in November 1931, the Abnormal Importation Act was passed. It provided that duties of up to 100 per cent ad valorem could be imposed on any manufactured article. A separate and coincidental act was passed for individual agricultural products. Three sets of tariff changes were issued under this act during November and December, imposing duties of 50 per cent on a wide range of manufactured items. The rationale for this policy change is hard to determine. The suspension of a month before had accomplished almost all of the aims of the tariff. The countries that were co-devaluators were not those countries which were the main object of the legislation. Contemporary discussion alluded to the fact that English merchants strongly expected upward tariff revisions if the nationals won the election. Therefore, it was alleged that the tariff was enacted to prevent the rapid increase in imports which would have been forthcoming in anticipation of this

38. 19.7 per cent into NICE, 32.8 per cent into Europe.

tariff. Thus, we have a self-fulfilling prophecy in the extreme.[39] If the government was, in fact, aware of rapidly increasing imports in late October and early November, and then reacted with a tariff, the only conclusion that can be drawn is that the government was extremely simple-minded or extremely devious.

An alternative rationale is offered by Britain's expectation of continental retaliation to devaluation. The enacting of protective tariffs in anticipation of a retaliation to your own previous actions is analogous to shooting your unarmed neighbor in self-defense, and then handing the wounded a pistol. Perhaps the answer lies in the political framework of the time. Given that the party in power was protectionist, it may have viewed the addition of tariffs to suspension as a double surety. Given that the crisis was occurring during a period when Britain was adhering to a policy of free trade, perhaps the British government thought that the abandonment of free trade, along with gold, would remedy the situation. At least public sympathy for free trade was lessened. A public willing to accept (however tacitly) the end of a structured international monetary system would accept in the same vein the change in commercial policy.

By February 1932, the turn to protection was formalized by the passage of the Import Duties Act, which placed a minimum duty of 10 per cent on all imports. It replaced the duties ordered under the Abnormal Importation Act, but all other duties remained. An Import Duties Advisory Committee was established and this body, beginning in April 1932, recommended higher duties on a number of articles. In particular, manufacturing duties were raised to 20 per cent, luxury goods to 30 per cent, and iron and steel products to 33⅓ per cent. A clause in the measure exempted all Empire products from these duties.[40]

Imperial preference may have been a contributory cause of the retaliation that was witnessed on the continent. With the passage of the Import Duties Act, eighteen European nations asked Great Britain to negotiate commercial treaties.[41] There are two possible explanations for the fact that these countries were asking for negotiations with Britain in the face of British suspension. One is that British trading influence with the continent overrode all other con-

39. Benham (3).
40. Ibid., pp. 31–34.
41. Condliffe (12), pp. 300–308.

siderations, and the other that the European countries were being more reasonable in terms of commercial policy. In the light of previous history, we must accept the former explanation.

The British government postponed all trade discussion on the grounds that trade agreements with the rest of the Empire were about to be initiated in Ottawa in the summer of 1932. Continental Europe was correct in anticipating a continued and/or increased preference on imports from the Empire. The Ottawa Conference formalized the discriminatory importation of Empire goods through the imposition of tariffs and quotas. The Ottawa agreements had five major clauses, all of which were of interest to European countries.

The first clause included the continuance of the pre-1931 free list for Dominion products. This list included over 80 per cent of Dominion exports to Britain. In addition, there was the promise that the remaining imports would face duties no higher than pre-1931 levels for three years. Any revision after that time would be undertaken along with a complementary change in duties or quantitative restrictions facing non-Empire countries.

The second imposed new duties ranging from 10 to 20 per cent on imports of certain foodstuffs originating outside the Empire. These included commodities previously imported without duty but of interest to Dominion exporters.

In the third clause, England agreed to keep the duties of February 1932 at a minimum of 10 per cent for at least five years. The fourth and fifth clauses included some specific quotas and prohibitions on the importation of classes of foodstuffs and agricultural products from non-Empire countries.[42]

This complete rejection of MFN agreements, and the discrimination against Europe especially, opened the door to a massive reaction in terms of restrictive policies. The combination of restrictive commercial policy and suspension had made very clear Britain's abandonment of free trade. Europe was entering a period of retaliatory policy which would begin with increased duties and continue through quantitative restrictions, exchange control, mixing requirements, clearing arrangements, and finally the reduction of international trade to barter.

Beveridge, quoting Pigou on reciprocity and free trade, stated in

42. Ibid., pp. 311–16, 185–87; Benham (3), pp. 71–109.

his classic plea against protection: "The advantage which a policy of freedom possesses over one of Protection does not, and never has been believed to depend upon its being reciprocated. . . . Gain through freeing imports from taxation does not depend on other countries doing the same. For other countries to tax our exports to them is an injury to us and an obstacle to trade. For us to tax their exports to us is not a correction of that injury; it is just a separate additional obstacle to trade."[43]

This perfectly reasonable statement of a second-best situation would have brought forth the prediction that a rational Europe should not have responded to England's change in policy. However, the European nations had several arguments which were reasonable to them which militated toward reaction. They included several separate arguments concerning restrictions for both external and internal stability, and a weaker argument concerning restrictions to be used as bargaining tools, to be removed later. This latter justification is analogous to military escalation for the purposes of attaining a negotiated peace, with essentially the same results. Rather than concluding that the continental nations were irrational in their responses, a better interpretation is that they were overwhelmed. While it had been difficult for free traders in England to convince policy-makers of the essential truth of Pigou's statement, it was asking too much to think that this view would be accepted in Europe where free trade was never an accepted policy and while Europe was facing the abandonment of that policy by its former staunchest ally.

As mentioned, there were a large number of commercial policy changes which affected both the intensity and the type of restriction employed. In addition, there was a proliferation of explanations regarding the purpose and necessity of the restrictions.

Continental reaction.—By 1930, France had combined tariffs and commercial treaties in order to establish a formidable protective policy. This protection became less effective in the face of falling world prices, sterling devaluation (France remained in the gold bloc), and the political constraints involved in renegotiating commercial treaties which had clauses tying tariff rates. The weakening of French protection and France's continued desire to restrict imports led to a major change in policy.

In 1931, France abandoned the tariff and established quotas as a

43. (4), p. 109.

method of import control. Quotas are a more serious trade restriction than tariffs. With quotas, the home country is completely severed from market-price interaction. Therefore, all equilibrating influences of trade are lost. Whereas the tariff had driven a wedge between internal and external markets, quotas had severed the link. During the second half of 1931, new quotas were placed on approximately fifty major items; by the middle of 1932, the number had risen to over 1,100 items; by 1934, over half of French imports (3,000 items) were covered by quota restrictions.

France was not the first nation in Europe to adopt quotas. They were also used in Austria, Czechoslovakia, and Hungary before 1931 but not to the extent that they were used in France. In 1931, Spain and Bulgaria had also adopted quotas, and by 1932 their use had spread to Germany, Greece, Netherlands, Poland, Roumania, and Switzerland.[44]

A corollary restriction to quotas is the granting of import licenses. If the licenses are sold competitively, the governments should be able to return to themselves the revenue loss induced by the change in policy from tariff to quota.

In order to have a quota-like effect on the importation of raw materials and foodstuffs, milling and mixing restrictions were employed. These restrictions operated by setting minimum percentages of domestic inputs into a production process. The most common case was flour production, where several countries (France, Germany, Finland, Sweden, Netherlands, and Italy) had a minimum percentage of domestic grain. During the early thirties, these minimums reached levels ranging between 75 and 80 per cent in most countries, hitting a high of 97 per cent in France. We can only speculate why this particular method was used. Perhaps governments caught between a political desire to protect agriculture and the demands of the populace for cheaper bread thought they could hide the quota in the input requirements.[45]

Germany's tariff reaction was strongest in foodstuffs, substantial in semimanufactured goods, and nonexistent in manufactures. Liepmann's (28) disaggregated German data reveal a percentage change in tariff levels between 1927 and 1931 ranging between 185 and 221 per cent for foodstuffs, between 52 and 81 per cent for semimanufactured goods, and between −3 and +5 per cent for manu-

44. Condliffe (12), p. 212.
45. Isaacs (18), pp. 645–46.

factured goods. Since other sources report no essential tariff changes for Germany after the commercial treaties in 1927 and before the crisis of 1931,[46] we can conclude that the figures represent the reactions to external changes. While it is true that Germany had a history of protecting agriculture, which these data seem to confirm, she did not abstain from restricting industrial imports. However, the method was not via tariffs, but rather through exchange control and bilateral trade.

Exchange control, a process whereby central banks impound foreign exchange receipts from exports and then dole out the exchange to importers in a restricted manner, can only be a constraint to the extent that the process supplants an existing foreign exchange market or to the extent that an alternative market does not develop. In the smaller agricultural countries (Bulgaria, Estonia, Latvia, Portugal, Turkey), exchange control was prevalent because exchange markets were small and dominated by central banks. The industrialized economies which were employing exchange control had to contend with the alternative of black markets in foreign exchange. The development of black markets appears to be related to the degree of exchange restriction, the penalties imposed, and the enforcement apparatus.

Of the major European nations which instituted exchange control in 1931 and 1932 (Spain, Germany, Hungary, Czechoslovakia, Yugoslavia, Austria, Denmark, and Roumania), Hungary is a good example of a regulatory system that failed. Data on the actual value of imports compared to foreign exchange allotted by the central bank over the period October 1931–December 1932 range from a ratio of 2.1 to 7.6. In Denmark, the control system began to break down due to an "inflation" in the size of foreign exchange requests tendered by importers. Requests for exchange during 1932 averaged over 150 per cent of the total import value of the previous period, and while only 25 per cent of the requested exchange was granted, this development made the task of efficient allocation of the rationed exchange almost impossible.[47]

Returning to Germany, we see an exchange control system which was apparently very successful. In early 1932, Germany installed a general system of exchange control with the avowed purpose of restricting imports. The initial restriction was 75 per cent of previous

46. Liepmann (28), p. 384.
47. Heuser (16), pp. 213–16.

years' exchange flow. This restriction was tightened to 65 per cent in March, 55 per cent in April, and finally 50 per cent in May.[48] The effectiveness of the operation is illustrated by a 69.6 per cent drop in imports between 1931 and 1932.

Germany in 1933 began to employ another policy approach to trade restriction, bilateral exchange via clearing arrangements. Exchange control and clearing arrangements are highly interdependent since the latter, in addition to being a separate measure, can be used in part to ameliorate the effects of the former.

Clearing arrangements are specific forms of commercial treaties where two countries agree to the price and quantity of goods traded and to the method of their payment, if any. A country which has instituted exchange control has not only restricted the flow of current imports (given the success of limitation) but any and all past commercial indebtedness will be frozen, since importers are just as restricted in their ability to procure foreign exchange for the purpose of paying old debts as they are for the purpose of buying new imports. The controlling country is in a position to strike a trading bargain with its creditor. An exchange of goods will be negotiated with a certain percentage of the debtor's exports allocated for past debt service and the remainder currently being paid for by creditor country exports. This process would circumvent some aspects of the exchange control by bypassing exchange altogether and substituting goods clearance. In an effort to regain some of the probable exporter losses to creditor countries, most nations undertook some form of clearing operations. Britain was the predominant creditor operating clearing agreements between 1932 and 1934, along with Roumania, Turkey, Hungary, Spain, and Yugoslavia. In 1934, Britain concluded the Anglo-German payments agreement, which was a more flexible clearing arrangement than an agreement based on exact and specific commodity transactions. Germany agreed to limit her British imports to 55 per cent of the value of German exports to Britain the month before. This enabled British exporters to minimize the length of time current receipts were tied up due to German exchange control.[49] This arrangement still left unsettled the pricing aspects of bilateral agreements and the general disruption to trade from the decline of multilateral trade.

The decline of multilateral trade was the offshoot of exchange-

48. Isaacs (18), p. 374.
49. Benham (3), pp. 127–28.

control-dominated bilateralism. Nonmultilateral trade was the expressed purpose of those clearing arrangements which were in fact strict barter. It is obvious that some of the exchange and/or payments-clearing arrangements were constituted by barter to a large degree. This aspect of trade arrangements was engineered by countries which were attempting to improve their balances of trade by the technique of both favoring trade with other countries with which they had had surpluses and by negotiating trade agreements whereby goods are traded without monetary agreements and, therefore, with no effect on the balance of trade. Every country could maintain a positive or zero trade balance through the use of barter, only at a lower level of trade. Barter-type trade agreements were conducted by a large number of countries between 1932 and 1934. Some of the larger agreements were in eastern Europe where raw materials and foodstuffs were bartered on a regular basis. In December 1932, Hungary and Czechoslovakia entered into commodity trading which resulted in Hungarian eggs and pigs being exchanged for Czechoslovakian coal. There were other notable trades between Sweden and Austria, Sweden and Hungary, Roumania and Yugoslavia, France and Bulgaria, Yugoslavia and Hungary, Italy and Roumania, Sweden and Italy, and Germany and all of Europe, concentrated in eastern Europe.[50]

During this period German trade policy began to take on aspects of autarchy. In manufacturing, radically improved trade balances and a change in the composition of trade, coupled with an evident change in the political composition and geographic location of Germany's trading partners, reflected Germany's turning toward a totalitarian commercial policy. This German trend would run against the trend of somewhat improved conditions of trade and policy during the recovery preceding World War II.

By 1935, every country in Europe was using almost every known method of trade restriction: tariffs, quotas, exchange control, devaluation, clearing and payment agreements, licensing of imports, mixing and milling restrictions, and barter. Embargo was even employed in the case of gold movements. The only significant restriction not employed was blockade, a policy which would have to wait for the years just preceding war for its use. Even the most stable European economies reverted to restriction during this period. Switzerland, which had a stable protection policy through the turmoil at the end

50. League (47), 2:200–202.

of World War I, undertook drastic changes after 1931. These changes included abandonment of MFN clauses, quotas, clearing arrangements, and exchange leverage. As she was a gold bloc country, this last policy constituted effective use of the Swiss currency in commercial treaties.

The Netherlands, the only continental holdout for free trade during the immediate pre– and post–World War I period, was also swept along by the restrictionist movement. In 1932, all existing tariffs were raised by 25 per cent and several new ones were enacted.

By 1935, Europe had descended to a historical nadir in trade and commercial policy. Total European imports and exports had dropped by 64 and 65 per cent, respectively. From this low, Europe was to begin a slow and uncertain recovery, which was also short lived.

RECOVERY IN THE WEST, GERMANY IN THE EAST

The second postdepression period, approximately 1935 to 1938, was dominated by a reduction of restrictions; there was a movement toward recovery of trade in western Europe and the emerging dominance of German commercial policy in eastern Europe.

Among the western countries, the continued existence of the two distinct currency groups had put pressure on the establishment of normal relationships since the abandonment of sterling. The gold bloc countries, by trying to maintain pre-1931 parities, had intensified their perceived needs for restriction. First Italy, in 1934, and then Belgium, in 1935, joined Britain in leaving gold. In September 1936, France, along with the Netherlands and Switzerland, dissolved the gold bloc and devalued. France had been suffering from adverse balance of payments, fleeing capital, and an increasing CPI because of British devaluation and French trade restrictions. By the middle of 1936, devaluation was being strongly considered. However, in an attempt to prevent the round of repercussive retaliations which followed British devaluation, the French government, in a unique example of cooperation and foresight, entered into negotiations with Britain and the United States concerning devaluation of the franc as part of an international trade agreement. The resulting Tripartite Agreement, issued on September 25, 1936, allowed for the mutual cooperation of French, British, and U.S. exchange stabilization funds for the express purpose of minimizing exchange rate fluctuations and promoting trade. In addition, the franc would be devalued and

France would reduce all duties and quotas by a given percentage.[51] This policy change did in fact stifle most repercussions except, of course, among those countries which were previously part of, or related to, the gold bloc. Switzerland and Netherlands had not intended to devalue, but the heavy gold drains on their national banks caused them to reverse their policy. The guilder and Swiss franc were devalued by 20 per cent and 30 per cent respectively, and the French franc by 30 per cent. Greece, Latvia, Roumania, and Turkey took independent devaluations and Czechoslovakia, which had been somewhat tied to gold in spite of extensive exchange control, devalued by 16 per cent.[52] These minor readjustments aside, the agreement stood as the most significant move toward international cooperation during the interwar period.

Preceding the Tripartite, England had engaged in some lesser trade agreements which had been made in the direction of looser restrictions. In June 1934, Britain and France were engaged in a battle over French quota assessments on British goods. Britain, claiming that the quotas were discriminatory against a set of U.K. goods, placed an additional 20 per cent surtax on all French imports. Subsequent negotiations removed the surtax and France reallocated quotas in proportion to predepression import levels. The British-Polish trade agreement of 1935 caused Poland to reduce duties on British textiles in return for a limitation of restrictions on the British import of Polish dairy and pork products. These agreements appear to have been closer to readjustments of the restrictionist policies rather than a movement toward improved trade relations. Two British agreements, with Denmark in 1936 and with the U.S. in 1938, show a marked trend toward improvement.[53]

France was unable to maintain a unidirectional move toward relaxed controls and several duties were raised after the Tripartite. By the middle of 1938, France had reduced restrictions again; sixty quotas were removed (one-fifth the number in force at the time), and it appeared that a permanent improvement in French policy was materializing. Certainly, France was reacting in part to the political developments in Germany and perhaps the trade policies were a visible sign of a political movement toward England and the U.S.

51. Isaacs (18), pp. 371–72; League (47), 6:8–11.
52. League (47), 6:11–13.
53. Benham (3), pp. 130, 134, 140.

By 1936, Switzerland had an extensive quota system with a quota on almost all foreign products. She had clearing arrangements with at least ten nations and a tariff structure which had not been changed since the early thirties. With the Swiss devaluation the government took a significant move toward reduction of restrictions. Almost all quotas were removed and tariffs reduced. Switzerland was also suffering from a reduction of exports to Germany, who had been her largest market between 1932 and 1935, and the second largest (next to the U.K.) before 1932.

For Netherlands, like Switzerland, Germany was a large market for exports, the largest market between 1932 and 1934, and second to the U.K. before 1932. Netherlands attempted to relax restrictions after devaluation but the Crisis Import Act of 1938, a reaction to the shrinking German market and domestic inflation, resulted in new quota restrictions, mainly on agricultural products. Netherlands was the only significant case in western Europe which did not show some improvement in trade controls.

The shrinking of German imports from the west was part of a new commercial policy which had its roots in the political change in Germany following the advent of the Nazi Party. When German commercial policy after 1933 is viewed as a part of her preparation for war, the isolation of Germany from the industrial markets of western Europe can be seen as a military flanking operation. It was the movement of a supply column inside friendly lines, rather than a move toward autarchy. The establishment of a viable exchange control, given Germany's dominant economic position in eastern Europe, enabled her to pursue a new mercantilism where the goal was not specie but a safe trade area for essential raw materials and foodstuffs. Clearing agreements, the complement to exchange control, were negotiated with increasing frequency by Germany in eastern Europe. With blocked mark flows, she was able to negotiate differential exchange rates among various trading partners and controlled the determination of the product mix of these "colonized" nations. By 1937, 50 per cent of German trade, and higher percentages of Bulgarian, Greek, Hungarian, Yugoslavian, Roumanian, and Turkish, was conducted via clearing arrangements and barter. Condliffe, in 1940, summarized German totalitarian commercial policies with this forceful rhetoric: "Every aspect of this trading system bears the mark of totalitarian methods. Thrusting the financing of trade on to the financially weaker countries, depleting their foreign exchange reserves, depreciating their external credit, pressing down the external value of their currencies, spoiling their export markets by the dumping of surpluses, and raising their domestic price levels, Germany was playing for much more than a mere temporary advantage in current trade. In the totalitarian conduct of trade policies, by using the methods of discriminating State monopoly, the German authorities were doing much more than establish a 'bilateral equalization' at the expense of the German consumers. They were, in fact building a new trading system, the center of which was the German *military economy*—a bilateral system in which all the traffic should flow to and from the center. This system was not designed to broaden into multilateral interchange in which there would be room for all the great trading countries to co-operate. It was designed to supplant and destroy the world trading system that Great Britain had built up and that the United States was trying to revive. Its methods are best understood when compared with those by which great monopolistic corporations have attempted, by horizontal and vertical integration, to destroy the trade of their competitors. In such struggles for power full use is made of discriminatory prices, dumping, massive raw material purchases, and even of terrorism. While the struggle is in progress, the smaller traders who supply materials or purchase the finished products may gain substantial advantages; but the achievement of even a partial monopoly advantage by one of the great competitors is apt not only to deprive them of such advantages, but to put them in a position where they must pay tribute."[54]

In commercial policy, as in politics, eastern and western Europe were on different paths that would meet in World War II. Germany's restrictive policies increased rapidly as she approached war. The recovery of trade in the West was also halted by the war. Moreover, the prewar conditions were so dominated by the impending military activity that a different analysis would be needed to continue the investigation. The depression, as the major influence on commercial policy, had run its course by the end of 1938.

SUMMARY

World War I and the subsequent peace left Europe with a set of conditions which made a return to prewar commercial policies im-

54. (12), pp. 252–56.

possible. In Britain, a postwar attempt at relaxation of restriction was short lived. French and German commercial policies were only beginning to move toward mutual reconciliation and lessened restriction by the time of the depression. All of the rest of Europe followed the general trends of the major nations in the postwar period. The slow and halting process of international reform in trade relationships up until the depression was such as to make impossible any recognizable trend in policy which would have occurred in the absence of the depression crisis.

The complete collapse of commercial policy into full-scale restriction was a reaction to outside stimuli, namely British policies and the general financial collapse at the onset of the depression.

Though the question of the true initiating cause of the round of retaliations is not crucial, it would be interesting to consider some alternatives. We have already looked at the possibility of the U.S. tariff as an initiating cause, and dismissed the direct effects. The indirect effects of the tariff, while possibly having been influential in European policy decisions via some expectational relationship, cannot be measured.

Another possible initiating cause of retaliation was American actions in the area of international attempts to create trade cooperation. Kindleberger (25) points to the American noncooperation at the Lausanne Conference in 1932, and the subsequent failure of the conference to enact any form of international cooperation, as the main reason for Europe's turn to aggressive restriction. This is within the context of Kindleberger's larger thesis that the depression in Europe was the result of a failure in leadership among several members of the international financial community. The thesis is, in its simplest form, that Britain could no longer provide that leadership, even if she had been willing, and that the U.S. was not willing, even though she was the only country which could have provided that leadership and the resources which leadership required. It is doubtful if even the U.S. could have stemmed the tide of the European restriction. Protective policies pre-dated World War I in Europe and were constantly employed in reaction to domestic economic crisis.

Only this complete set of postwar conditions could have created the unstable equilibria whereby any shock would have sent Europe on its course of trade destruction and retaliation. It mattered little which shock it was. It could have been any one of several, between

1930 and 1932. Britain's commercial policies are a reasonable reference point, but had it not been one particular cause, it would have been another.

The formal model, which will be used later for estimation, and the historical investigation were determined jointly. While the history of the period implies that a macroeconomic-trade model would be appropriate for studying a period of rapidly changing income among highly interconnected nations via trade, the model itself influenced the choice of focus in the historical survey. The one set of variables, commercial policy variables, which was crucial for the estimation of such a model, was to a large degree unavailable. The attempt to overcome that loss was the main reason for concentrating on a history of commercial policy in the first part of the study.

The diversity of policy actions, both in type and in intensity,. leads us to include among the questions about changes in trade flows, changes in preferences concerning trade, and changes in policy, which we will answer in the later chapters, some questions about flows, preferences, and policies as sources of differentiation among subgroups of countries. The subgroups arise from the postwar conditions and structure of the European economy. The relationships of debtor and creditor countries, industrial and non-industrial countries, eastern and western European nations, and continental countries and the United Kingdom all show subgroups of European countries which may have had different patterns of behavior during the period and different reactions to the depression. The history poses questions as well as providing answers.

The actual data output, in terms of commercial policy, comes in three distinct forms: tariff level data, qualitative restriction data, and exchange rate data.[55] Each type can be subdivided into two groups: the first consists of continuous series or overall data for a large number of countries; the second comprises isolated levels, rates, and/or actions of individual countries.

The tariff level as an index of the overall percentage of ad valorem tariff rates is unavailable as a continuous series. However, there are data on a group of countries for specific dates. What is needed to reconstruct the overall tariff rate for any country in any year is the complete set of tariffs on all goods and the complete disaggregation of imports by all goods. This disaggregate information is not avail-

---

55. All available data are reproduced in the Appendix.

able. Some studies have been attempted, based upon less than complete data. The earliest attempt to construct such rate indices for the post–World War I period was undertaken in a League of Nations study in 1927 (45), which provided tariff level indices for 1925. The other major study is by Liepmann (28), who calculated tariff level indices for 1927 and 1931. With the addition of some countries whose tariffs were more or less constant on all goods, a fairly complete list for a large number of countries is available for the three years mentioned. In addition, the history provides a large number of tariff rates and their changes for individual goods and years. This information will complement the remaining qualitative policy data. There were many changes in nontariff policies during the post–World War I period, especially during the depression. While these data cannot be quantified, they can be timed, and both overall and individual changes in policy can be ranked to produce an ordinal measure of tariff and nontariff restriction.

Exchange rate data are available as a continuous series throughout the period in the form of an index of the current price relative to par of any country's currency.[56] While normally thought of as a market measure, this series can more logically serve as an additional policy variable. Before 1931, exchange rates were fixed and any fluctuations were minor, moving to the gold points only. After the sterling crisis, when one or more countries floated their currency, the changes in the rates, especially on a yearly basis, were dominated by devaluation rather than market fluctuation. In addition, exchange control would tend to hide the market variation. Therefore, the exchange rate series, plus the available individual information on single country devaluation, provide an additional commercial policy variable.

The combined output of this section will be used as input into these aspects of the remainder of the study: tariff level calculations of foreign trade multipliers, tariff and nontariff ordinal variables, exchange rate variables, timing of a priori breaks in the postwar period, grouping of nations for tests among various propensities, choice of exogenous and instrumental variables in estimation, tariff, quota, and budget data for use in determining revenue aspects of restriction.

56. League (41).

3

The European Flow of Trade

A COMPLETE intercountry matrix of trade flows is not available as a continuous series during the interwar period. However, there is a matrix for three of the period years, 1928, 1935, and 1938.[1] Fortunately, these dates are dispersed and provide reference points for before and after the crisis period (1930–31) and a recovery end point. Merchandise, import, and export data for the entire world, by nation, are shown. The values are reported as local currency converted into post-1933 dollars. This allows comparability and includes all effects of devaluation.

Since this study deals with Europe, I will consider only the European portion of the matrices (see Appendix, Table 24). As mentioned, data limitations constrict the analysis of Europe to twelve sample countries. For comparison, most of the analysis here will deal with this group.

These twelve countries can be divided into three subgroups: industrial continental Europe (ICE), nonindustrial continental Europe (NICE), and the United Kingdom. The problem with the first two divisions is that it is not clear which nations belong in each group.

At this point, I will refer to the disaggregation given by League classifications, but I will return to the question of alternative groupings in a later section. The League classification placed Belgium, Czechoslovakia, France, Germany, Netherlands, Sweden, and Switzerland in the first subgroup, and Bulgaria, Denmark, Finland, and Hungary in the second. The first represented 81.5 per cent of total European exports in 1928, and 78.8 per cent of imports for the same period. The remaining countries, mostly agrarian and in eastern Europe, while representing a small portion of total European

1. League (40), (43).

trade, accounted for an extremely high percentage of intra-European trade. During the period between 1925 and 1930, these countries' trade, averaging 83.5 per cent of exports and 78.0 per cent of imports, remained inside Europe.[2] In addition, the whole group, except for the United Kingdom, had an intra-European trade percentage of 80.3 per cent of exports and 71.4 per cent of imports, respectively, thereby strengthening the validity of the assumption that we can study continental Europe as a closed economy.

The trade flow data do not clear to a total, i.e., the sum of any one country's exports does not necessarily equal the sum of all other countries' imports from it. This fault is due to the problems of port-of-entry evaluations and trans-shipping. Where trans-shipping data are recorded, a separate listing of "special" trade is provided.[3] This discrepancy will introduce a bias into the data. However, the necessary assumption that trans-shipping moves in proportion to regular trade is probably not a gross violation of fact. The basic data have been recalculated to include trade balances and percentage changes in exports (X), imports (M), and the balance of trade (B). Table 24 (Appendix) records X, M, and B for all group nations disaggregated by their sources. Tables 25 and 26 (Appendix) present percentage changes in X, M, and B, respectively, for the twelve countries.

What can we infer from this body of data? We cannot accurately ascertain the exact relationship between commercial policy and trade. The first reason for this is that the data are too sparse in a time sense to infer that any change in trade flow between two countries can be aligned with a particular policy condition. Such an analysis would require monthly data at best and yearly data at a minimum. A second reason is that even if such a body of data were available, simple comparisons of policy with trade cannot assign all of the trade change to the policy. A model is necessary to specify the impact of divergent and concurrent economic variable change. The second qualification is the most cogent, and will be dealt with explicitly in the econometric model.

What I shall be investigating in general are the crude tendencies for trade values to change in a predictable fashion between the reference points. The predictability, i.e., the a priori expectations

2. Liepmann (28), p. 412; League (43).
3. League (43).

of the changes, will be tested in reference to, and be the result of, the insights of history and theory.

THE MOVEMENT TO INCREASE THE BALANCE OF TRADE

For a number of reasons, both internal and external, all of the countries of Europe after 1930–31 attempted to improve their balances of trade. If the success of interwar policies is to be judged by the ability of the various countries to achieve this goal, then between 1928 and 1935 the policy attempt must be considered a success. Nine of the twelve group countries increased their balances along with a total of twenty out of twenty-four European countries.[4] The three countries from our sample group for which total trade balances declined during the period were Czechoslovakia, France, and Sweden. Czechoslovakia and Sweden were partially successful in their efforts to improve their balances of trade (B). Both countries had positive balances with the rest of the countries in the group. Their balances improved in the second period (1935–38). France was the only country to suffer a negative effect in its total balance. She also suffered this loss within every major geographic subdivision, and failed to improve her balance in the second period. Perhaps the extremity of France's restriction, in both harshness and type, brought forth an equally strong retaliation. Trade balance decreases ranged from 50 to 100 per cent on average.

Was the policy of improving trade balances justifiable by European nations at that time? For any individual country, an improved balance is usually considered beneficial. In a Keynesian model, increasing the trade balance is equivalent to an upward shift in the X–M schedule. The assumption that this upward shift will generate a new equilibrium at a higher income level, regardless of the aggregate level of exports, is fallacious for decreases in X and M. What is assumed is that the loss of X with an even larger loss of M will lead to higher domestic incomes because of a transfer of resources and production out of the external economy into the internal economy. This is a different mechanism than the one implied for trade balance improvements which result from improved exports or from lowered imports only. These latter cases involve an absolute increase in domestic production. Without retaliation, higher exports are a

4. Ibid., pp. 112–62.

direct increase in income, whereas lower imports should stimulate production of import substitutes.

In the presence of retaliation, i.e., the case of falling imports and exports, aggregate domestic production declines. The presumed increases in import substitutes are supposed to be greater than the production loss from falling exports simply because the quantity of import decline exceeds the decline in exports. This simple analysis disregards all consideration of the relative demand elasticities of exports and import substitutes. Moreover, within the context of price distortions in international trade, the resource transfer from exports to import substitutes cannot take place in such a manner as to yield the same output as before the change in trade balances.[5] In addition, if the reallocative mechanism is imperfect due to domestic distortions, the loss in income will be even larger.

We can see that the policy to improve trade balances was a reasonable response by European nations only if they were convinced that the policy would be free from retaliation, and if they also thought that the major improvement in balances would arise from export improvement. It is difficult, at best, to believe that the European nations held these views. A cursory knowledge of the history of European commercial policy and a knowledge of the degree of interconnection of European trade were sufficient to have indicated that retaliation, rather than being the exception, would have become the rule.

Without even considering the general effects of retaliation upon exports, most countries faced a situation where import restriction dominated export improvement. For each country it was true that the attempt to improve (B) was most easily accomplished by a unilateral reduction in imports. This fact can be substantiated by noting the preponderance of import-restricting policies and the paucity of export-improving policies during the period. Improvement of exports was difficult. Most countries, seeing the market for their own exports as fairly autonomously determined, and seeing themselves as a small part of the total market, looked upon exports as exogenous. Among the policy restrictions generally employed, only devaluation had some aspect of export stimulation. Germany, being

5. This is in welfare-indifference terms, i.e., relative prices change and production of export and import substitutes takes place at a new point on the production possibilities curve, whose relative price line cannot intersect the old indifference curve. See Bhagwati (5).

a large seller to part of Europe, did employ the use of some export bounties and credits, but this use was small when compared to her use of policies to restrict imports.[6] While we may wonder at the self-destructive aspects of trade-balance-improving policy in the face of this, we cannot argue with its existence.

Almost all of the nations of Europe were able to increase their trade balances at lower levels. The unfortunate result was that they thereby produced lower incomes. Every group country had a reduction in exports and imports between 1928 and 1935. This reduction averaged 59.8 per cent for exports and 62.0 per cent for imports. The almost equal percentage reductions in X and M are deceptive. Had the reductions been of an equal percentage, a pre-condition of an import surplus would have yielded an increase in the balance of trade. Europe in 1928 had an overall trade deficit of $6.841 billion, or 26.7 per cent of exports. The previous deficit, combined with the slight relative percentage reduction in M, explains the overall improvement in trade balance to a deficit of $2.590 billion in 1935, an improvement in (B) of 62.1 per cent.

Given the overall trend of improving balances and declining imports, was there any differential behavior, in terms of trade flows, among countries? Were there sets or groupings of countries by characteristics which may provide insights into their trade behavior?

An examination of the structure of the pre-1930 intracountry debt indicated that it was necessary for debtor countries to secure foreign exchange for the payment of debt service which had been lost due to the financial crisis. The attempts to secure exchange by these countries caused them to move quickest and to the largest extent toward securing positive or improved balances. Table 1 shows the group divided into three debt subgroups, debtors, neutrals, and creditors.[7] For debtors, the marked upward percentage changes are contrasted with the deterioration of balances for all the creditor countries until the first and second halves of 1931. It appears that up until the retaliatory policy changes, sparked by Britain's leaving gold in 1931, the debtor countries were successful in improving

6. Isaacs (18), pp. 758–60.
7. Yearly data, League (41); semi-annual data, League (47), 1:172. Division by debtor, neutral, creditor was problematic for France and Belgium, who were net debtors to the U.S. and U.K., net creditors to the rest of Europe, and net creditors overall. This last fact plus the financial crisis in Germany and Austria were taken as the deciding factors in placing them on the creditor list.

TABLE 1
PERCENTAGE CHANGE IN TRADE BALANCE BY COUNTRY
1928–38

	1929 I	1929 II	1930 I	1930 II	1931 I	1931 II	1935	1938
DEBTORS								
Bulgaria	−40		300		−110		(130) −200	167
Czechoslovakia	−98		2550		− 23		(−72) − 32	121
Germany	62	88	368	496	− 11	144	(106) − 94	−215
Hungary	95		450		− 73		(113) 183	120
NEUTRALS								
Sweden	216		−514		−172		(−25) 43	33
Denmark	19		− 24		0		(64) 64	46
Finland	81		229		500		(129) − 17	−110
CREDITORS								
Belgium	− 27	− 57	− 55	80	− 29	86	(4) −783	23
France	−396	+ 59	− 69	− 27	31	31	(−286) 3	− 22
Netherlands	42	− 14	3	22	− 2	13	(64) 19	− 50
Switzerland	37	− 30	0	− 41	26	− 29	(15) 23	59
United Kingdom	37	− 7	6	− 7	8	7	(53) 28	− 39

NOTE: Trade balances are total X–M. 1929I–1931II semi-annual data are annualized. Yearly data corrected by exchange rate and discounted into dollars (000,000). Percentage change from previous year except for ( ) from 1928.

trade balances. Germany, starting with a 62 per cent gain in its balance in 1929 (from −815 to −308) had, by the second half of 1930, achieved a positive balance (382) and an almost 500 per cent gain over the preceding period. By 1931, this growth was slowed; by 1935, the balance had dropped to 6 per cent of its 1931 level. This 1935 level was still positive and larger than the 1928 level. The United Kingdom shows mixed changes in its trade balance throughout the period, with the only substantial gains occurring after 1931. At the very least, the debt structure affected the timing of countries' movements toward improving trade balances. Another implication of the debt structure was that debtor countries might alter their trade balances in order to incur export surpluses with their creditors. This concept, investigated further in the discussion of bilateralism, can be roughly examined by the use of trade flow data. Countries may pursue a bilateral movement in hope of securing an overall balance and/or as a reaction to exchange control. In Table 2, I compare the average import reduction for each debtor nation with the individual and average reduction of that country's imports from each of the debtor nations. Only Bulgaria and Germany exhibit the indicated behavior. The debt effects of Czechoslovakia and Hungary appear to have been swamped by import reductions from Germany. Also, the comparison period is too long. Ideally, we would look for a peak in the effects of debt upon trade between 1932 and 1933. Table 1 exhibits positive debtor balances falling between 1931 and 1935. We know that restrictions peaked by 1934–35. Therefore, the low significance levels can be attributed to the reference points as well as to the data.

It appears from the history that there was a distinct favoring of protectionist policy in the face of crisis. This trend was more pronounced in some countries than others, as can be seen by policy actions before 1930. There appeared to be no such distinction among the policies of various countries during the depression. An investigation of the import behavior of four countries (France, Germany, Netherlands, and United Kingdom), representing the extremes of protectionist and free trade nations respectively, reveals that in terms of the operational measure of the trade restrictions, there was no measurable historical bias. Even if we were to ascertain that the attitudes of these countries toward protection were different,[8] given that they undertook protectionist actions, we could only infer a historical bias in their commercial policies if the realizations of the protectionist policies they enacted were different. That is to say, did a historical trend toward or away from protection alter the degree of restriction of imports?[9] The flow data are presented in

8. After 1931, it was not different in the U.K., and even if different in the Netherlands, the Dutch government acted as if it were not. Policies were undertaken which, though not as severe as in some other European countries, were for the Netherlands a large change in the level of restriction.

9. Granting that the predepression free bias of the U.K. and the Netherlands was removed in policy, was there any vestige of that old policy so as to mitigate the impact of the restrictions?

TABLE 2

CHANGES IN IMPORTS 1928–35 FOR GROUP COUNTRIES
(000,000)

	Group $\overline{\Delta}$M	Creditor $\overline{\Delta}$M	Belgium $\overline{\Delta}$M	France $\overline{\Delta}$M	Neth. $\overline{\Delta}$M	Switz. $\overline{\Delta}$M	U.K. $\overline{\Delta}$M	T. Stat.[a]
Bulgaria	— 2.0	— 3.4	— 3	— 6	— 1	0	— 7	d
Czechoslovakia[b]	— 39.1	— 15.4	— 8	— 25	— 2	–16	— 26	+
Hungary[b]	— 13.4	— 5.6	— 2	— 7	— 4	–10	— 5	+
Germany	–122.3	–201.4	–140	–315	–208	–87	–257	3.11
(%Δ)[c]								
Bulgaria	— 45.5	— 82.5	–100.0	— 85.6	— 50.0	0	— 77.8	7.04
Czechoslovakia	— 57.6	— 60.4	— 53.3	— 61.0	— 14.3	–66.7	— 61.9	+
Hungary	— 68.7	— 64.9	— 66.7	— 77.8	— 57.1	–71.4	— 40.0	+
Germany	— 65.8	— 74.3	— 73.3	— 81.4	— 72.5	–65.4	— 71.4	1.12

a. On group $\overline{\Delta}$M and creditors $\overline{\Delta}$M, individual creditors will exceed or fall below this test statistic.
b. ΔM from Germany –308 and –43, respectively.
c. Averages weighted by ΔM dollars.
d. + are not significantly different from zero.

Table 3. By far the most striking feature of these data are their similarities. Only the declines in nonindustrial Europe by U.K. and Germany are significantly different[10] from the overall European decline of 64 per cent. This only compounds the conclusion that the quality of being a free trader before the depression did not hinder the ability to restrict imports afterward.

Between 1928 and 1935, the dichotomy between eastern and western Europe grew. The four eastern countries in the sample (Bulgaria, Czechoslovakia, Germany, and Hungary) reduced their imports by an average of 66.5 per cent. The comparative reduction of the western subgroup was 59.3 per cent. However, the small variance for the group as a whole (1.823 per cent) indicates that the difference in import declines was significant at the .001 level. The difference in percentage changes was still significant between

TABLE 3
PERCENTAGE CHANGE IN IMPORTS
1928–35

| | Protectionists | | Free Traders | |
	France	Germany	Britain	Netherlands
Group	−64.7	−70.1	−61.2	−65.5
Ice	−63.8	−70.9	−72.1	−64.7
Nice	−65.4	−53.5	−54.4	−61.0
Total	−60.8	−70.6	−68.9	−65.2

1928 and 1938 (better than 0.10 level). However, if Bulgaria is omitted (because of a lack of information concerning the extent of Bulgarian barter), the percentage decline differential of 13.7 per cent is significant at the .0005 level.

There will be other tests of this dichotomy in the bilateral section. A first approximation indicates that the east-west dichotomy, which was present in policy after 1933, had an effect on trade levels. An analysis of Germany's direction of trade changes shows us that eastern European trade was recovering at a slower rate than western European trade. Moreover, it was evident that there was a shift by Germany away from western Europe toward eastern Europe. Between 1928 and 1935, exports to, and imports from, ten of the eleven group countries trading with Germany declined. Between 1935 and 1938, exports increased for eight of the eleven group countries, and imports increased for nine. It is interesting to note

10. T test on the difference between means from the same population.

that for the second time period, trade values improved for all of Germany's eastern neighbors but improved only for five of the eight western countries in exports and six of the eight western countries in imports. In 1938, France, United Kingdom, and Switzerland were importing fewer German goods than in 1935, and France and Switzerland were exporting less to Germany than in 1935. The conclusion that Germany turned from the west is reinforced by the increase in German imports from the east by 33.3 per cent compared to a 21.4 per cent increase from the west. This is an underestimate of the intensification of the isolation of German trade, since many clearing trades which were actual barter may not have been recorded in the League statistics.[11] Clearly, there was a relatively higher increase in trade. Some of this has been captured by the flow data. Other portions of it may have been lost due to the inability to capture all the relevant data concerned with barter.

We have looked at some disaggregations of trade values in order to answer questions about the trade response of various subgroups. We have not looked at the industrial-nonindustrial or the continental–United Kingdom differentials. These will be discussed later. The industrial-nonindustrial differentials will reappear in the econometrics. The influence on trade from general tariff and nontariff restriction is harder to enumerate with this body of data. We do have tariff level measures for 1927 and 1931, and we can assume that, until the latter date, tariffs were the major restriction. Therefore, we have a cardinal measure of policy to compare to gross trade performance. However, after 1931, we can only conclude that it was the sum of tariff and nontariff restrictions that was impinging on trade and this sum can, at best, be represented by an ordinal measure of policy. Moreover, the matrix reference points of 1928 and 1935, respectively, bracket the period where almost all of the differentiation in the timing of different restriction ranks occurs. We can only attempt to match individual policy changes between countries with those countries' mutual trade flows. This procedure, too, is marred by the spacing of the reference points.

BILATERALISM

There are many forms of bilateralism, the policy of trading with countries on a one-to-one basis in order to secure favorable trade

11. (43), p. 110.

balances. These include exclusive trade with countries with which a given country previously ran surpluses, clearing arrangements or barter which bypass the trade balance, and payments arrangements which are reactions to exchange control. All of these operations were documented in chapter 2. Bilateral trade can at best have no effect upon a previous multilateral free trade equilibrium only if that trade equilibrium was bilateral beforehand.[12] This case did not exist in Europe in 1928, as can be observed by the number of positive and negative trade balances for every European country regardless of the overall balance. Since that time, almost all nations had attempted to reduce the degree of multilateral trade. Table 4 shows

TABLE 4
PERCENTAGE OF TRADE BALANCE WITH COUNTRIES
WITH WHICH CLEARING ARRANGEMENTS HAVE BEEN MADE

	1931	1932	1933	1934
France	69.1	58.6	82.1	95.6
Switzerland	42.7	55.6	48.6	55.9
Italy	33.4	66.6	67.3	81.2
Hungary	36.9	45.0	50.9	83.6
Bulgaria	3.7	67.3	28.4	46.2
Roumania	59.3	83.8	28.8	89.8

the relative portions of trade balances of several European countries divided between those countries with which they had concluded clearing arrangements and those with which they had not.[13] Except for Bulgaria and Roumania between 1932 and 1933, there is no challenge to the trend away from multilateral trade.

We can study the effect of bilateralism upon trade flows by considering its effect on the dispersion and the predictability of trade patterns.

Bilateralism, through cleared trade balances or barter, alters the size and variability of trade balances. Consider the vector of balances for any country. As bilateralism progresses, the probable size

12. This is a simple extension of the effect of constraints upon a general equilibrium system. The system is only unaffected by the constraints if the constraints are not binding. In my example, the constraints of bilateral trade would only have been nonbinding if the unconstrained solution were bilateral. Since the predepression 1928 solution was not bilateral, the imposition of bilateralism was a constraint that must have brought the new output/utility level solution below the old level. Bilateralism must have contributed to lower trade levels. See Friedman (14).

13. League (47), 3:186–89.

of any surplus or deficit will decrease. Bilateralism will reinforce the tendency toward balanced trade since the nations will seek out barter, which removes the trade from the deficit or surplus. The effect of barter will be to reduce the balance size by the value of the bartered goods. Therefore, the variance of the vector of trade balances between the first two reference dates should contract. Any differential in bilateralism among groups of nations, between the first and second set of reference points, should be observable in

TABLE 5
INDICES OF TRADE BALANCE VARIATIONS, GROUP COUNTRIES
(1928 = 100.0)

	Ib_{1935}	Ib_{1938}	Ix_{1935}	Ix_{1938}	Im_{1935}	Im_{1938}
Belgium	24.9	41.2	37.5	41.8	32.2	37.1
Czechoslovakia	15.7	17.6	16.8	20.7	16.3	14.0
France	21.6	18.2	20.9	19.7	31.9	27.3
Germany	17.9	16.4	20.8	19.3	20.4	21.2
Netherlands	37.6	47.3	30.3	35.8	32.8	33.3
Sweden	26.9	29.6	47.3	69.3	41.3	59.3
Switzerland	39.7	32.1	40.1	35.6	48.7	37.4
Bulgaria	76.8	22.6	170.2	91.2	147.9	106.2
Denmark	18.5	21.3	37.8	44.7	33.6	40.9
Finland	37.2	46.3	65.6	84.4	22.1	37.5
Hungary	15.5	17.0	68.1	89.4	27.2	36.9
United Kingdom	21.8	26.0	32.6	34.0	27.7	31.2

NOTE: Subscripts b, x, m refer to indices of trade balance, exports, and imports variances respectively. Indices were calculated by setting 1928 standard deviation equal to 100.0.

the variances of trade balances between any country and all other countries. In Table 5, I have constructed an index of the variances of trade balances for all intragroup trade.[14]

Trade variances fell by a substantial amount for all group countries. Germany, Czechoslovakia, and Hungary reached the lowest levels for both periods. This reconfirms the conclusion of differential bilateralism discussed in chapter 2. France, Germany, Switzerland, and Bulgaria were the only countries to have a continuance of variance contraction after 1935. France's loosening of restrictions after 1936 does not appear to have altered the dispersion properties of her trade. For the group as a whole, the general contraction of

14. The standard deviation of each group country's import, export, and trade balance vis-à-vis other group countries. Index of standard deviation constructed so that 1928 = 100.0.

variances is startling. The degree to which extreme balances with other group countries had declined was obviously the result of the restrictionist policies in Europe which were directed at reducing deficits. This movement toward the reduction of deficits and the general trend toward balanced trade arrangements should also have been manifested in a reduction of variances about imports and exports. These data, also shown in Table 5, have variances reduced for eleven of the twelve countries. Germany and Czechoslovakia have the largest dispersion contraction for exports, Germany has the largest for imports.

A change toward bilateralism should alter the pattern of trade in a predictable fashion. Consider 1928 as a free trade base year and 1935 and 1938 as bilateral years.[15] We would expect an improvement in the relationships between the first and second years' patterns of trade (the degree to which the 1935 trade resembles the 1928 trade, and similarly for 1938 and 1935). Bilateralism implies directed or planned trade. Therefore, market variables would be expected to have a lessened influence on the pattern of trade in the second period than in the first period. Political and administrative policies, operating through bilateralism, would tend to solidify the pattern of trade once these lines were established.

Table 6 shows simple correlation coefficients for each country's intragroup trade values for 1928–35, 1935–38, and 1928–38. This last statistic should indicate whether the deterministic aspect of bilateralism increased or decreased between 1935 and 1938. Consider a comparison of the 1928–38 correlation with the 1935–38 value. If the latter exceeds the former, this indicates that there was a smaller effect of bilateralism in the second period. Since bilateral negotiations would affect both sides of the market, these tests were run for both imports and exports. The comparisons were also run for trade balances. Countries successful in achieving trade balance goals would tend to continue similar trades through bilateralism. In terms of trade balancing, France had the strongest showing with a .414 increase in the simple correlation of individual trade balances (Rb). France's attempts to discriminate in trade in favor of those countries which improved the French balance altered her pattern of surpluses and deficits. Both Germany and Hungary show a large increase in the stability of their trade balance patterns. The

15. While this may not be true from a free/protection point of view, it is reasonable concerning bilateralism.

TABLE 6
GROUP COUNTRY TRADE FLOW CORRELATIONS (R, SIMPLE)
(1928, 1935, 1938)

	$b_{28}b_{35}$	$b_{35}b_{38}$	$b_{28}b_{38}$
Belgium	0.328	0.368	0.261
Czechoslovakia	0.923	0.308	0.280
France	0.560	0.974	0.627
Germany	0.736	0.921	0.857
Netherlands	0.976	0.966	0.985
Sweden	0.980	0.898	0.877
Switzerland	0.811	0.943	0.922
Bulgaria	0.126	−0.273	0.601
Denmark	0.998	0.993	0.991
Finland	0.786	0.976	0.707
Hungary	−0.393	0.938	−0.265
United Kingdom	0.733	0.943	0.747
	$x_{28}x_{35}$	$x_{35}x_{38}$	$x_{28}x_{38}$
Belgium	0.940	0.897	0.854
Czechoslovakia	0.933	0.986	0.932
France	0.980	0.988	0.965
Germany	0.880	0.948	0.900
Netherlands	0.985	0.982	0.951
Sweden	0.992	0.981	0.956
Switzerland	0.931	0.964	0.976
Bulgaria	0.959	0.996	0.966
Denmark	0.995	0.997	0.999
Finland	0.953	0.988	0.972
Hungary	0.588	0.993	0.550
United Kingdom	0.826	0.982	0.801
	$m_{28}m_{35}$	$m_{35}m_{38}$	$m_{28}m_{38}$
Belgium	0.986	0.998	0.986
Czechoslovakia	0.977	0.989	0.970
France	0.991	0.992	0.987
Germany	0.874	0.823	0.523
Netherlands	0.999	0.995	0.993
Sweden	0.973	0.998	0.971
Switzerland	0.979	0.996	0.986
Bulgaria	0.874	0.993	0.879
Denmark	0.751	0.996	0.793
Finland	0.799	0.990	0.824
Hungary	0.734	0.996	0.728
United Kingdom	0.909	0.980	0.846
	$x_{28}m_{28}$	$x_{35}m_{35}$	$x_{38}m_{38}$
Belgium	0.890	0.945	0.878
Czechoslovakia	0.977	0.979	0.951
France	0.938	0.891	0.909

TABLE 6—*Continued*

Germany	0.719	0.913	0.770
Netherlands	0.885	0.846	0.736
Sweden	0.722	0.896	0.925
Switzerland	0.794	0.979	0.896
Bulgaria	0.858	0.994	0.992
Denmark	0.591	0.952	0.951
Finland	0.541	0.814	0.812
Hungary	0.984	0.986	0.990
United Kingdom	0.809	0.906	0.904

NOTE: b = trade balance; x = exports; m = imports.

Czechoslovakian statistics indicate a counterhistorical result. However, the major cause for the changed trade balance pattern was a German-Czechoslovakian deficit for the first time. The change in German-Czechoslovakian trade flows may have been war related. Only five of twelve countries show an improvement in trade balance correlations between the two periods, while nine out of twelve had an improvement in exports, with the other three accounting for very small changes. The generally higher Rb in the West compared to the East for 1928–38 is consistent with the history of continued bilateralism in the East and a loosening of negotiated trade in the West.

Import correlations, like exports, show an overall rise in the second period (ten out of twelve countries increased). The evidence of a solidification of trade patterns is stronger here. Again, for the comparison of 1935 and 1938 bilateralism, Czechoslovakia and Hungary show increases in imports and exports, while Germany shows these increases for imports only. While we do not presume that a free trade 1938 equilibrium would necessarily mimic the 1928 equilibrium, a greater fit between 1928–38 than 1928–35 might show the degree to which relaxation may have moved the 1938 solutions more toward the 1928 level than the 1935 level.

An additional test of the balancing of trade goals plus the degree of predepression multilateralism is garnered by calculating the correlations between imports and exports across countries for any given country in each year (Rxm). Multilateralism should exhibit a looser fit than bilateralism. If trade is planned and also one-to-one, exports and imports will align themselves to a greater degree than in the case of unplanned trade. Table 6 also shows these results. Rxm improves for ten of the twelve countries between 1928 and 1935, while declining for nine of the twelve countries in the 1935–38 period. The growth in Rxm between the first two dates indicates an overall average increase of almost 25 per cent in the percentage of trades which were matched. The increase for Germany was almost 50 per cent.

Bilateralism was prevalent throughout Europe during this period. The extent of the activity was even more predominant in eastern Europe. We must complete the picture of the European trade structure by delineating partially disaggregate inter- and intraregional patterns of trade. Furthermore, we must attempt to answer some questions concerning the effect of policy activity upon this structure.

THE MAJOR LINES OF TRADE

In attempting to depict the general lines of trade flow for Europe, some upward aggregation from the level recorded in Table 24 is necessary. At this level we will be able to depict the major changes in the pattern of trade between the reference points.

Europe's trade was highly self-contained, especially that of the continent. Industrial continental Europe (ICE) imported over 50 per cent from inside Europe (56.1, 58.3, and 56.0 per cent in each reference year) and exported almost 70 per cent to Europe (70.9, 68.8, and 67.6). Nonindustrial continental Europe (NICE) was even less open, importing 73.7, 75.9, and 79.1 per cent from inside Europe while it exported approximately 85 per cent to Europe (85.7, 84.9, and 86.6). This distribution of trade remained roughly constant over the 1928–38 period with only the steady increase in NICE's internal imports exhibiting a clear trend. Figure 1 depicts the pattern of trade between NICE, ICE, and the rest of the world (ROW). For NICE, the dominant trade feature was trade with ICE. NICE's ICE imports represent 52.0, 46.1, and 50.8 per cent of NICE's total imports. ICE's trade is more open, although internal trade plus NICE trade represent a large portion of the flow. At this level, there did not appear to be any significant distributional changes. The trade levels declined substantially: an average of 65 per cent overall for 1928–35, and an increase of only 17 per cent overall in 1935–38. The one clear trend that does emerge was the steady decline of intra-ICE trade. Most of this movement was in industrials, which were restricted to the largest degree. The two largest traders in ICE were France and Germany. Their share of intra-ICE trade declination was consistent with the history of trade restrictions.

The openness of continental trade is exaggerated by the inclusion

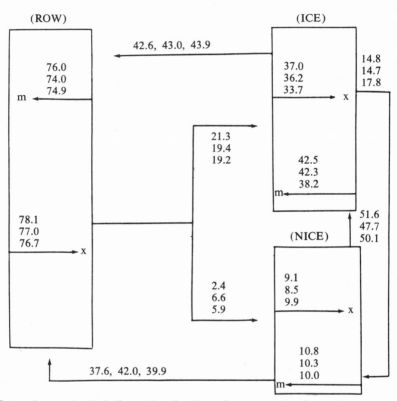

External arrowheads indicate the direction of exports only. Internal arrows indicate intragroup trade, left-headed (m), right-headed (x).
All numbers are in percentage terms from box of origin for 1928, 1935, 1938, respectively.

Fig. 1. Industrial continental European (ICE), nonindustrial continental European (NICE), and rest of the world (ROW) trade flows, 1928, 1935, 1938

of the United Kingdom in ROW. In Figure 2, we depict the trade flows, including U.K., NICE, and ICE in European trade. Most of the external continental trade is directed to the U.K. and most of the external European trade leaves via the U.K. The continent formed a link with England, whose trading size and markets allowed her to become a substantial part of European trade and still conduct 70 per cent of her trade with ROW. This structure suggests a possible pattern by which intercountry reaction may take place. Consider ICE and NICE reacting to the U.K., and the U.K. relating to the outside world. The only exception is that some of the NICE countries with a very high percentage of their trade with ICE will react to ICE rather than to the U.K. This is the structure employed in the estimation stage of the econometric model.

The Ottawa agreements in 1932, whereby England added heightened imperial preference to her restrictive policies toward Europe, would have been expected to shift the U.K. trade flow away from ICE and NICE and toward ROW. Even though the first two reference points miss the timing of the effects of the Ottawa agreements by three years, there was some increase in the U.K.'s import percentage from ROW. Where ROW's share of exports to Europe rose by 1.3 per cent, the share to the U.K. rose by 3.3 per cent, a net share gain of 2 per cent or almost $400 million in increased ROW imports. The U.K. also decreased her import share from ICE by 1.7 per cent and increased her share from NICE by 3.5 per cent of each group's exports. The existence of a higher previous level of trade between the U.K. and ICE was sufficient to cause total U.K. importation from the continent to drop by $80.1 million.[16] Since total trade dropped drastically for England during this period, there was an implied redistribution of British trade within ROW. These were realized by a large drop in U.S. shares by almost 5 per cent and smaller drops in Africa and parts of Latin America with substantial share increases for Canada (2.7 per cent) and Oceania (4.4 per cent). It appears that the Ottawa agreements had as much effect in redistributing U.K. trade within ROW as in discriminating against ICE.

Intra-ICE trade was dominated by France and Germany. In Figure 3, the intra-ICE trade pattern reveals some of the results of policy.

16. Dollar values of the per cent change in trade flows calculated on the average trade between periods. These are dollar changes relative to initial positions and are not actual observed trade quantities.

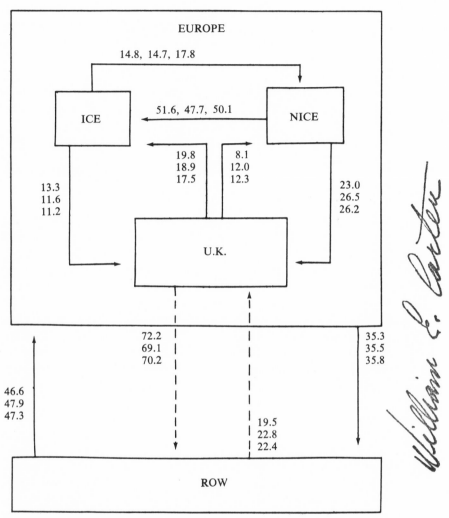

Arrowheads indicate direction of exports in percentage terms from box of origin, 1928, 1935, 1938, respectively.

Fig. 2. ICE, NICE, ROW, and U.K. trade flows, 1928, 1935, 1938

The trade war between France and Germany is obvious in the rapid fall in trade shares between them. There was a loosening of Franco-German relations between 1927 and 1929 due to the signing of commercial treaties. Therefore, there exists the possibility that the first reference point was atypically high. Nevertheless, the decline continued from 1935 to 1938.

France and Germany had very different experiences with intra-ICE trade. France accepted higher import shares from the rest of industrial continental Europe (ROICE) while her export share dropped. Germany radically improved the share of her exportation to ROICE while receiving a smaller portion of ROICE's exports. Perhaps French quotas and coefficients were less effective than German exchange control and barter.

The data in Figures 1–3 provide a picture of trade interactions in Europe. Moreover, some of the more prominent trends in commercial policy appear to have been verified by changes in the trade pattern. We are unable to infer very much more about tariff-like policy from the data. The availability of only three reference points made statistical tests impossible where percentage changes were being compared across time. But even without the aid of tests, we can be fairly confident of the pattern which has emerged, especially the interaction between the United Kingdom and the rest of Europe.

We have been able to isolate a few tests of commercial policy, i.e., to show that a plausible set of trade reactions to policy was not inconsistent with the data. The effect of commercial policy upon the general pattern of trade and trade dispersion was very large. The effects of individual policy changes have been difficult to establish, due primarily to the wide time spans between reference points. The emerging pattern of trade flows has been useful in describing a pattern of trade reaction.

We have moved from a study of policy to a study of trade and attempted to link them. Before attempting a modeling of trade–income–commercial policy relationships, let us consider the trade-income relationship. Having established the latter by gross measures, we would attempt an estimation of the parameters of a model which formally link the three factors. Knowing full well that a model does more than just formalize, i.e., it constrains the data so as to provide meaningful implications from coincidental events, we consider gross measures as a first step in our understanding to be used as a complement to later results.

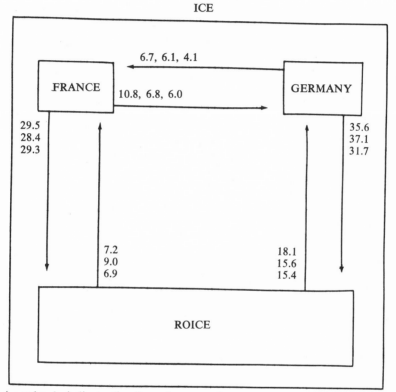

Arrowheads indicate direction of exports in percentage terms from box of origin, 1928, 1935, 1938, respectively.

Fig. 3. Intra-ICE trade flows: 1928, 1935, 1938. France, Germany, and rest of industrial continental Europe (ROICE)

GROSS MEASURES OF INCOME LOSS FROM TRADE DESTRUCTION

Earlier in this chapter the effect of trade activity upon income was discussed. A joint measure of trade activity is needed because this level cannot be measured by imports, exports, or the trade balance alone. The average trade activity (R) will, at this point in the investigation, allow us to calculate trade as a portion of income generated in a sectoral fashion.[17] Relating R to Y provides a measure of the

TABLE 7
TRADE/INCOME PERCENTAGES
1924–38, 1929–31

	1[a]	2[b]	3[c]	4[d]
Belgium	39.2	50.3	42.4	65.1
Bulgaria	10.6	47.2	12.5	19.2
Czechoslovakia	19.5	30.6	24.8	204.1
Denmark	28.7	57.7	31.0	88.0
Finland	28.0	45.6	45.6	65.7
France	18.4	16.2	19.1	116.2
Germany	12.5	16.3	15.7	27.7
Hungary	15.5	25.1	18.4	36.4
Netherlands	33.5	74.5	35.1	79.0
Sweden	18.6	34.3	19.6	61.2
Switzerland	21.3	41.2	23.4	75.8
United Kingdom	18.1	42.0	19.3	63.6

a. $\bar{R}/\bar{Y} \times 100$ average of all values 1924–38, overall level relationship.
b. $\Delta\bar{R}/\Delta\bar{Y} \times 100$ fitted from regression 1924–38, overall change relationship.
c. $\bar{R}/\bar{Y} \times 100$ average 1929–1931, depression level relationship.
d. $\Delta\bar{R}/\Delta\bar{Y} \times 100$ average change annualized 1929–31, depression change relationship

$$R_i = \frac{(X_i + M_i)}{2}.$$

difference in the trade and income relationship between the entire interwar period and the depression impact period.

There are two qualities of trade and income proportions that are measured. The first relationship concerns the relative sizes of trade activity and income. Trade was a major source of goods in Europe. Over the complete period, mean R/Y ranged from a low of 10.6 per cent for Bulgaria to a high of 39.2 per cent for Belgium (see Table 7). The group mean was 21.4 per cent and the median was

17. $R_i = (X_i + M_i)/2$; this measure tells us the average portion of trade activity appropriate for comparison with Y_i, $i = 1 \ldots n$. The trade balance X–M does not give us level information and the gross trade activity X + M double counts the trade level.

slightly higher than 19 per cent. There is only one division of the group which was indicated by a ranking of values in column (1). This is an east-west division with Germany, Hungary, and Bulgaria being the three lowest ranked nations.

The second measure is relative change. The knowledge that trade was a substantial part of income was the first step in assigning a role to trade in income change. The second step concerned the measurement of the portion of the decline in income which was assignable to the decline in trade. There is a superior method for analyzing the portion of the decline in income which was the result of trade rather than the use of mean percentage changes in R/Y. A more representative value can be determined by fitting a simple constrained regression between R and Y, over the period, allowing for an intercept shift at the depression.[18] These estimates of the proportion of income change accounted for by trade are consistently higher than the overall level relationships. Trade was a larger part of the fall in income than the proportion of trade in income in eleven out of twelve cases.[19]

Trade activity is a sizable portion of income levels and changes. The relationship is intensified when measured across the depression impact dates. The mean R/Y levels and the calculated R/Y percentage changes for the depression dates are higher than their corresponding values for the entire period 1924 to 1938. Trade represented both a larger part of income, and a larger portion of the decline in income when the general contraction began. The essential ranking of countries is unchanged for the shorter period with the same three countries having the lowest average R/Y values. The short period weighted average is 24.1 per cent and the median is almost 22 per cent. At a minimum this coincidental measurement yields a value of between 20 and 25 per cent for the trade loss and income loss relationship.

Woytinsky's data (34) on the share of exports in industrial production for total-world-averages represent another measure of the

18. $\Delta R = b_1 \Delta Y + b_2 \binom{0}{1} + e$, dummy at 1930 or 1931, estimated by Hildrith-Liu. $b_1 \times 100 =$ "average" percentage change in R for a percentage change in Y over the period. Table 7, col. 2.

19. We cannot use cols. (1) and (2) in the common relationship of average to marginal propensity, since these results are not propensities but simple proportions. The implications of multipliers and linkages is evident. The multiplier model which will be developed later has validity in the coarse data as well as in theory.

size of trade relative to income.[20] Export trade quantities dropped by almost 20 per cent more than the overall drop in production after the depression. Woytinsky states that European trade reduction was greater than the world average. Liepmann's data (28) on exports and production[21] confirm this contention. By 1934, British trade had dropped 31 per cent more than production, and in Germany, the loss in trade was 44 per cent greater.

It appears that trade was undergoing heavy contraction along with income during the depression, hardly a startling result. We have seen that the measure of trade related to income is sizable. A comparison of R/Y for both full period and depression period between group countries and the U.S. (4.95 per cent overall, and 4.85 per cent for 1929–31)[22] reveals both a higher trade proportion in Europe and an increase in the level of R/Y in Europe during the depression; this did not occur in the United States.

However, even the large size of European trade relative to European income cannot, by itself, confirm that income change is caused by trade. In order to establish causality, it is necessary to isolate the role of trade in a model of macroeconomic behavior. The commercial policy information of chapter 2[23] and the trade flow information of chapter 3 will be used to aid in the estimation and specification of such a model. That there was cause to consider trade and income relationships was in part evidenced by these gross measures.

20. (34), p. 43. He also has data from which R/Y can be generated but for 1949 only; these were calculated and are reproduced here for reference:

Belgium	35.7
Nether.	31.7
Finland	31.6
Denmark	25.4
Switz.	21.4
Sweden	21.3
U.K.	19.7
Czech.	17.3
France	15.2
Germany	11.1

21. Page 375.
22. Woytinsky (34), p. 62.
23. All compiled data from chap. 2 are presented in chap. 4 and Appendix.

4

An Econometric Model of European
Income and Trade

Among the forty-two volumes referred to in Cheng's extensive review (10) of empirical trade studies concerning the interwar period, only three deal with trade and income relationships in Europe.[1] There were no major studies written after the publication of Cheng's summary in 1960.

Chang's study (9) of balance of payments includes estimates of marginal propensities to import (MPM) for ten of the countries in our group. His estimates are derived from sample regressions of imports on income, prices, and time. The use of a trend variable improves the fit of Chang's regressions at the expense of explanation. The effects of all other economic variables upon imports, where those variables increased or decreased together in time, are hidden by the inclusion of the time variable. There are other technical faults in Chang's work. His price and income deflator is an index based upon exchange rate levels. Exchange rates were fixed for the first half of the interwar period and were flexible for only a small number of European countries for the second half of the period. The rigidity which was present in exchange rates was not present in prices to the same degree. Moreover, exchange rate values after the depression represented policy actions rather than relative prices. The use of the wrong relative prices was compounded by Chang's use of a per capita income measure to explain total imports. These technical comments notwithstanding, Chang's work was the first approach to an estimate of the various MPM's for Europe in this period. His MPM estimates should be viewed in much the same way as the gross measures discussed previously, i.e., the MPM estimates will provide us with an initial and rough measure which shall be improved and refined by subsequent work. A more general criticism

1. All coefficients of previous studies are compared with the current results in Table 9.

of Chang's work is the absence of the qualities of explicit policy effects and intercountry interaction in his model. While the remaining two studies do not achieve complete success in terms of specification or estimation, they represent a vast improvement over Chang's first approach in 1951.

These two studies are superior efforts. The authors move a step beyond Chang, asking questions about country interaction, but their methods cause their results to fall short of their goals. Polak's (32) attempt to measure MPM's within the context of an international system fails because of the statistical properties of his estimates. While Polak discusses an interactive model, he in fact estimates single and independent equations for each country's imports. This process produced estimates which were of the same type as Chang's. Polak's model is a general approach to trade; imports are a function of income and prices, income is a function of exports and exogenous variables, and exports are a function of all imports. This could be the basis of a workable theory; however, Polak estimates each equation in turn by ordinary least squares. These are not estimates of a reduced form garnered from the three functional relationships (a method which is also problematic), but rather each function is estimated separately. All the information which could have been derived from interaction is lost. In addition, this form of estimation suffers from specification error. Additional problems are introduced into Polak's estimates by the use of a time trend. Furthermore, the scale of trade effects cannot be measured because he uses index numbers and not actual values for imports and exports. Polak's price variable is also questionable in that it is essentially an internal index. He divides the import good price index by the cost of living index, thereby yielding the price of importables relative to domestic goods. This is not the price of all goods at home relative to all goods abroad. This second measure reflects the impact of all foreign price changes while the former reflects to some extent policy actions which should be dealt with separately. Polak constrains his regressions through the origin, and therefore his reported marginal propensities are in fact averages. Nevertheless, Polak's work did point out that interaction between countries was a necessary part of the world trade model, even though he did not advance the process of estimating that interaction.

Neisser and Modigliani's work (30) antedates Polak by one year. Published in 1953, the work is a major step toward solving the conceptual problems of a multicountry trade and income model. It is a formidable study, with none of the obvious faults of the other works, but it does fail in certain aspects of estimation and concept. A major innovation of the work is the division of some of the countries' trade by product class. This improvement is costly in that only three countries had sufficient data to be identified individually after the disaggregations. Neisser and Modigliani group the data of the remaining countries into sectors determined by product class. Product classification provides answers similar to the results gained from my investigation of the relative behavior of various national subgroups. We cannot judge the benefits of disaggregation relative to the losses incurred by the elimination of estimates of individual country behavior. At best, we can observe that the disaggregation produces a loss of information about nations and an increase in the refinement of our information about countries within product groups. Unfortunately, these estimates are not free from problems of specification and estimation error.

Most of the major problems are the result of Neisser and Modigliani's assumption about the exogeneity of income. This assumption leads them to derive structural equations in which trade values are netted out. The estimation of the net relationships by ordinary least squares produces reduced form estimates relating import changes to exogenous income variations. If income is not in fact exogenous, then the income coefficients of the ordinary least squares equations are not the true MPM's (the direction of the bias will be discussed). The very nature of the specification error also causes the authors to omit policy variables from the estimation of import propensities. In a model of trade and income behavior where income is endogenous, it is necessary to include other variables which are exogenous and use these in the estimation process. However, the assumption of exogenous income precludes the search for other variables. The reduced form method used by Neisser and Modigliani can only return information about the structural equations under certain circumstances. While it would be unfair to ask the authors to have returned the structural coefficients of the trade and income relationships when they thought that income was exogenous, there did arise further interpretive problems because the reduced form estimates were not solved back even when it was possible to to return the implied structural coefficients. This study was impressive in its magnitude and exhibited a superiority both in the sophistication of the model and in the thoroughness and scope of detail. However, it did not have an integrated approach to policy and trade relationships. This was a direct result of the assumption of exogenous income.

I will now begin the description of a basic model of trade and income, following the path implied by previous works. In subsequent stages I will incorporate the concepts of income endogeneity, inter-country interactions, and policy determinants necessary to complete the model.

A KEYNESIAN TRADE AND INCOME DETERMINATION MODEL

Consider a simple Keynesian model with constant prices. Income is generated within national income accounting sectors. Consumption and import functions are stated separately. World commerce is typified by free trade.

$$Y = C + A + X - M \qquad (1)$$

$$C = C_0 + C_1 Y \qquad (2)$$

$$M = b_0 + b_1 Y \qquad (3)$$

$$Y_e = \frac{1}{(1 - C_1) + b_1} \cdot X^* + A^*A \qquad (4)$$

$$Y_e = m_0 \cdot X^* + A^*A \qquad (5)$$

Where: A = autonomous expenditure

A^* = autonomous expenditure multiplier

$X^* = X - b_0$, trade balance term

Y_e = equilibrium income

m_0 = minimum nonrepercussive foreign trade multiplier.

m_0 will be an approximation of the effect of trade upon income. A given change in the trade term (X^*) will produce an m_0Y change in income. The export component of the change is the result of an exogenous change in outside income.

A relaxation of the free trade assumption, by the consideration of the existence of tariffs, alters the equilibrium solution and therefore the size of the trade multiplier. Consider a government imposing import tariffs as the difference between internal and external prices. The government collects a tariff revenue equal to the tariff rate times the value of imports. We can include the effects of such a policy in the model without specifically relaxing the assumption of constant prices. Using the small country argument of exogenous external prices, we can infer that the tariff is fully affected at home. Therefore, the tariff revenue represents a tax upon aggregate import expenditure. We can replace the income term in the import equation by a disposable-income-for-imports term which represents the net income available for import expenditure, after collection of tariff revenues. Combining equations (1) and (2) with

$$M = b_0 + b_1(Y - T \cdot M) \tag{3'}$$

and solving (3') for M in terms of Y and T

$$M = b_0' + \frac{b_1}{1 + b_1 T} Y \tag{3''}$$

where: $b_0' = b_0/(1 + b_1 T)$

yields the following equilibrium:

$$Y_e = \frac{1}{(1 - C_1) + \left(\frac{b_1}{1 + b_1 T}\right)} X^{**} + A^* A \tag{6}$$

$$Y_e = m_T \cdot X^{**} + A^* A \tag{7}$$

Where: T = an ad valorem import tariff rate

$X^{**} = X - b_0'$, a tariff corrected trade balance term

= the tariff adjusted foreign trade multiplier.

This tariff inclusive model has an implicit assumption concerning governmental expenditure policy, namely, that the increase in general revenue as the result of tariff collections is not returned to the domestic economy in the form of expenditures. If the governments were to increase their expenditures by any amount as the result of increased tariff revenue, there would be an additional effect upon income resulting from that expenditure.[2] Since tariffs will affect the trade multipliers by different amounts depending upon assumptions of redistribution of revenue, we should investigate the probable effects of the expenditure of tariff revenues. The polar case with which we contrast this example of zero revenue expenditure is an assumption of an increase in expenditure equal in amount to the tariff revenue collected. Combining equations (2) and (3″) with an income equation representing full expenditure of tariff revenues

$$Y = C + A + X - M + TM \tag{8}$$

yields the following:

$$Y = C_0 + C_1 Y + X - b_0' - \frac{b_1}{(1 + b_1 T)} Y + T b_0'$$

$$+ T \frac{b_1}{(1 + b_1 T)} Y + A$$

and therefore,

$$Y_e = \left[\frac{1}{1 - C_1 + \frac{b_1}{(1 + b_1 T)}} + \frac{b_1 T}{1 + b_1 T} \cdot \right.$$

$$\left. \frac{1}{1 - C_1 + \frac{b_1}{(1 + b_1 T)}} \right] X^{***} + A^* A$$

$$Y_e = \frac{\frac{1 + 2b_1 T}{1 + b_1 T}}{1 - C_1 + \left(\frac{b_1 T}{1 + b_1 T} \right)} X^{***} + A^* A \tag{9}$$

$$Y_e = m_T^f \cdot X^{***} + A^* A \tag{10}$$

2. Johnson (19).

Where: $X^{***} = X + (T - 1) (b_0')$, a tariff corrected trade balance term

m_T^f = the tariff adjusted foreign trade multiplier where there is an increase in expenditure equal to the full amount of the tariff revenue.

To summarize, the model to this point has produced three foreign trade multipliers under varying assumptions about free trade and tariff revenue expenditure. The multipliers are:

$$m_0 = \frac{1}{(1 - C_1) + b_1} \text{ , free trade}$$

$$m_T = \frac{1 + b_1 T}{(1 - C_1)(1 + b_1 T) + b_1} \text{ , tariffs with no expenditure change}$$

$$m_T^f = \frac{1 + 2 b_1 T}{(1 - C_1)(1 + b_1 T) + b_1} \text{ , tariffs with full expenditure change}$$

Both m_T and m_T^f have the property that when $T = 0$, the multiplier values would equal m_0. While there is no upper bound to T, an analysis of the tariff levels during the interwar period indicates that a value of 1 was the upper limit in practice. This value of 1 has a computational advantage in that the expression for the difference between m_T^f and m_T can be easily expressed as:

$$b_1 T / [(1 - C_1)(1 + b_1 T) + b_1].$$

While the value of the difference between multipliers is zero or near zero, when tariffs are zero or near zero, the multiplier differentials, as a function of the expenditure assumption, are significant when tariffs are large. Without discussing estimation, the mean size of $m_T^f - m_T$ is approximately 65 per cent of the nonexpenditure multiplier. We will investigate the implications of available budget data upon the validity of either assumption (zero or full revenue expenditure) later.

Central to the estimation of the multipliers are tariff levels, consumption propensity, and the import propensity. The Keynesian import function does not include relative prices and the value of the MPM is constant over the income varying range. A superior specification would be to include price changes and propensity changes explicitly. In a world where prices do fluctuate, the specification of equation (3″) causes all of the effects of price change to be reflected in the measurement of the MPM. While the use of a dummy variable for a change in time period before and after the depression does not reflect changes in MPM, it does reflect a shift or change of scale variable. We will view changes in import-income relationships over the depression period, where the functions are correctly specified as being a change in taste. The first approach to an explicit price and taste change specification will be the estimation of

$$M = b_0' + b_1'Y + b_2P + b_3d \qquad (11)$$

Where: $b_1' = b_1/(1 + b_1T)$
        P = index of relative prices
        d = dummy variable across a predetermined "depression" date.

Since d will not capture the effect of changes in b_1 over the period, more sophisticated tests of that change will be employed in subsequent forms of this equation. Comparing (11) with (3″) demonstrates that tariffs will alter the estimated value of the MPM if the data do not permit retrieval of b_1. We are faced with this problem although estimates of the bias indicate that it is not severe.[3]

The tariff levels and consumption propensities will be taken as given, from other studies,[4] although at best these are estimates.

Returning to the model, the scope of the analysis has been a short-run cyclical Keynesian model. This structure omits several aspects of the effects of trade destruction. While some of the aspects will be tractable, others will be only mentioned.

---

3. An attempt to re-estimate MPM's for 1927–31 with a correction for the specification that $b_1 = b_1'/(1 - b_1' T)$ is performed; for the few dates available b_1 exceeds b_1' by at most 20 per cent, at minimum less than 5 per cent, on average less than 10 per cent.

4. Neisser and Modigliani refer to British and German consumption data for the period but they do not report the aggregates. The British data are superseded by Corbo's work (13). His results were derived from both a linear single year and distributive lag consumption function. I chose a value from the lagged technique which would be more compatible with post-Keynesian consumption functions. For the subperiod 1920–38, his value for the MPC (C_1) was 0.870 which was used in the calculations of the m_T's and m_T^f's.

An analysis of the effects of trade upon growth will have to be omitted. This is a dynamic question, not sufficiently dealt with in the literature. Most, if not all, studies concern themselves with the effect of growth upon terms of trade and then the effects of terms of trade upon trade. These involve, for the most part, analysis of the implications of growth of factors in a Hecksher-Ohlin model. There may be other effects of growth. Consider growth producing new products and industries, changes in income-price consumption patterns along the same preferences, and changes in the population mix. Modeling this range of activities is outside the scope of this study. Moreover, the literature (5, 9) also gives consideration to the possibility of immiserizing growth. Therefore, even if the trade and growth relationships were well defined, the relationship between growth and income would be ambiguous.

Trade destruction also affects optimality. Distortions and misallocations are present when trade is destroyed. These are not to be confused with the simple income loss resulting from a shrinkage of free trade. If world export production falls while there are no barriers to trade or if the desire for trade (taste) changes so that aggregate imports fall, there is no distortion per se; yet total welfare will have declined in the first case and may have declined in the second. These welfare losses are suffered while the system is still operating at Pareto optimality. However, if trade destruction is caused by barriers to free trade, then there are welfare losses incurred in addition to those measured by conventional income studies. Any inequality among domestic marginal rates of substitution and foreign marginal rates of transformation (trade at foreign prices) represents a certain welfare loss.[5]

These considerations, plus the impact of policy in a reactive model, reinforce the use of commercial policy variables as a necessary addition to the determination of equation (11). That specification will change as a result of the next set of considerations and therefore we postpone an explicit statement.

The model and equations discussed so far are not general equilibrium simultaneous structures. They fail to capture the essential interaction of trade functions among countries. These interactions work through income, prices, and policy. Using Polak's unestimated model as a starting point we can extend the model implicit in equations

5. Bhagwati and Ramaswani (7).

(1), (2), and (11) by considering a world of more than one country. Imports are still a function of own country income and prices.

$$M_i = b_{0i} + b'_{1i} Y_i + b_{2i} P_i \qquad (12)$$

Income for any country remains a function of internal, autonomous, nontrade components of national income (A') and the country's trade balance.[6]

$$Y_i = A'_i + X_i - M_i \qquad (13)$$

The countries are joined by a clearing equation among exports and imports and by corresponding import functions in each country.

$$X_i = \sum_{j=1}^{n} M_j^i \qquad i \neq j \qquad \begin{array}{l} M_j^i = \text{the imports of country } j \\ \text{from country } i \end{array} \qquad (14)$$

$$M_j = b'_{0j} + b'_{1j} Y_j + b_{2j} P_j \qquad (15)$$

Finally, the internal import price is a function of outside prices and policy variables. The latter is represented as tariff and nontariff restrictions (T) and exchange rate changes (EX) for the home country.

$$P_i = F(P_j, EX_i, T_i) \qquad (16)$$

The model composed of equations (12) through (16) describes a system whereby income, prices, and trade are endogenous while policy variables are exogenous and drive the model. This specification is consistent with the historical role of commercial policy restrictions. Equation (12) is identified and can be estimated using the exogenous policy variables and instruments.

$$M_i = b'_{0i} + b'_{1i} Y_i + b_{2i} P_i + b_{3i} EX_i + b_{4i} T_i \qquad (17)$$

The choice of instruments will be discussed. Equations (12), (15), and (17) have been written here without dummy variables; an alternative and superior technique will replace them in this form of the equation.

Estimation of the models will proceed from fits of equation (11)

6. $A' = C + A$.

and its variations to estimates of the coefficients of equation (17). Equation (17) should prove to be a superior structure. For the first time, trade interaction, commercial policy, and modern estimation techniques will be combined. All of the resulting coefficients will then be used to calculate various multipliers culled from alternative specifications of the tariff revenue assumptions. These will offer alternative measures of the effect of trade destruction upon income. In an attempt to isolate the causes of trade destruction an experiment will be conducted using the estimated equations from the general model. We will generate income values under alternative states of nature. Predicted values of income level during the period when policy, taste, or both remained unchanged will be compared to the fitted values using the actual data of the period. These comparisons should indicate the degree to which differing behavior contributed to income loss during the period.

Before turning to questions of estimation, there are data problems and conditions which will be examined first.

INPUT FROM HISTORY AND TRADE FLOWS: DATA AND INDIVIDUAL EQUATION SPECIFICATION

The varied output of the preceding chapters provides two basic types of information. First, data, both quantitative and qualitative, are used as variables in the estimation process and in the construction of multipliers. Second, the output of these chapters provides information about interconnections among various nations. This second set of information, along with information about the timing of economic events, will enable us to ascertain the optimal set of instruments for the estimation of the general model.

The data on tariff levels, culled from Liepmann (28), League (45), and Woytinsky (34), are reproduced in the Appendix. These data are available for only three dates during the period: 1925, 1927, and 1931. Since this is not a continuous series over the period we could not use the tariff levels as a variable in estimation. However, we were able to use tariff levels in the construction of multipliers representative of periods before and after the depression started.

The remaining body of tariff data is subjective. While the history of commercial policy does produce an understandable pattern of tariff levels and nontariff restrictions, by its nature, that survey cannot produce a quantifiable vector of commercial policy. Most of the information about a given country's policy is incomplete and applicable only to parts of the country's trade. The task of producing sensible restriction level indices from the data, which are presumably contained in individual country trade statistics, would necessarily be the subject of separate research. Without the individual national data the task would be impossible. However, quantitative data are not the only input which can be used. While we cannot compare the cardinal value of various restrictions between countries and across time, we can rank the level of restriction for any given year.

The choice of the number of ranking levels was severely limited by the estimation implications of the technique. Each level becomes a separate variable in the regressions (after the use of the constant as the first or zero level) and therefore uses up a degree of freedom for each level. This cost places a severe restriction upon the number of levels since degrees of freedom are scarce in short-period annual time series. My compromise between statistical restrictions and a ranking system which would adequately reflect the policy changes is a three-level ranking. This system is represented by two vectors of intensity with the constant absorbing the first level (see Table 8).

We can illustrate the method of construction of the ranks by tracing the choice of ranks for some sample countries. Remember that the rankings have no relevance as measures of restriction levels between countries, but only represent a measure of changing restriction intensity over time, within a nation.

For France, the major turning point for an already high postwar restriction policy was the use of higher level coefficients in 1930 and the use of a massive quota system beginning in 1931. France's level of restriction was reduced, but not to predepression levels, by the Tripartite agreement of 1936.

Germany's experience was typified by a large increase in restriction beginning in 1925 with the lapse of constraints upon her activities resulting from the Versailles Treaty. The next massive upward change in restrictive policy was the strengthening of her exchange control activities, an increase in bilateral trades, and the advent of other totalitarian policies, all dating from 1933. By 1935, German withdrawal from the West was well on its way, while her trade patterns in eastern Europe were stabilized. Though Germany's eastern trade was exploitive, it was an improvement over the absence of trade which typified the earlier period.

TABLE 8
RANKINGS OF TARIFF AND NONTARIFF TRADE RESTRICTION LEVELS

	Belgium		Czech.		France		Germany		Finland		Netherlands	
	TI	TII	TI	TII	TI	TII	TI	TII	TI	TII	TI	TII
1924	0	0	0	0	0	0	0	0	0	0	0	0
1925	0	0	0	0	0	0	1	0	0	0	0	0
1926	0	0	0	0	0	0	1	0	0	0	0	0
1927	0	0	1	0	0	0	1	0	0	0	0	0
1928	0	0	1	0	0	0	1	0	1	0	0	0
1929	0	0	1	0	0	0	1	0	1	0	0	0
1930	0	0	1	0	1	0	1	0	1	0	0	0
1931	0	1	0	1	0	1	1	0	0	1	0	1
1932	0	1	0	1	0	1	1	0	0	1	0	1
1933	0	1	0	1	0	1	0	1	0	1	1	0
1934	0	1	0	1	0	1	0	1	0	1	1	0
1935	0	1	0	1	0	1	1	0	0	1	1	0
1936	1	0	0	1	1	0	1	0	0	1	1	0
1937	1	0	1	0	1	0	1	0	0	1	1	0
1938	1	0	1	0	1	0	1	0	0	1	1	0

	Sweden		Switz.		Bulgaria		Denmark		Hungary		U.K.	
	TI	TII	TI	TII	TI	TII	TI	TII	TI	TII	TI	TII
1924	0	0	0	0	0	0	0	0	0	0	0	0
1925	0	0	0	0	0	0	0	0	1	0	1	0
1926	0	0	0	0	0	1	0	0	1	0	1	0
1927	0	0	0	0	0	1	0	0	1	0	1	0
1928	0	0	0	0	1	0	0	0	1	0	1	0
1929	0	0	0	0	1	0	0	0	1	0	1	0
1930	1	0	0	0	1	0	0	0	1	0	1	0
1931	1	0	0	1	0	1	0	1	0	1	0	1
1932	0	1	0	1	0	1	0	1	0	1	0	1
1933	0	1	0	1	0	1	1	0	0	1	0	1
1934	0	1	0	1	0	1	1	0	0	1	0	1
1935	1	0	0	1	0	1	1	0	1	0	0	1
1936	1	0	1	0	0	1	1	0	1	0	0	0
1937	1	0	1	0	0	1	1	0	1	0	0	0
1938	1	0	0	0	0	1	1	0	1	0	0	0

British policy changes fluctuated almost on an annual basis after the First World War. Within the time period of this study the first major change occurred in 1925 via an increase in tariff rates. The abandonment of sterling, along with increased protection, makes 1931 the next date to which to ascribe a substantial increase in restrictive policy. Finally, with the Tripartite agreement and individual policy changes, Britain in 1936 appeared to have returned to a level of restriction similar to that before 1925.

All of the other country rankings follow the same general approach as to their construction.

The other major series which provided a policy vector was the exchange rate index. As stated, this series was dominated during the interwar period by the drastic changes in rates which occurred during devaluation. Therefore, we can consider the series as a policy rather than a market measure. The League (41) reported average annual exchange rates by country in two separate ways, during the period before 1930 by a discount or premium on dollars and after 1930 by a percentage of gold parities. These two series were reconciled into a continuous exchange rate series for each nation over the period (see Appendix).

The budgetary data relevant for a choice of the proper tariff revenue assumption will be considered after we have discussed the construction of multipliers later in the chapter.

An exogenous variable which is not part of the policy group is the date when each country experienced the depression crisis. While this did not occur over any convenient annual period, the assignation of a date by year will be helpful for two purposes. First, that date will be used to test the change in MPM's of the import functions over the crisis. Second, the date will be used as an exogenous instrument representing an external crisis. The history of commercial policy plus two League documents provided the information necessary for the determination of the break year for each country.[7] An economic indicator measuring economic conditions gives turning points after 1929. In addition, the League documents provide a monthly listing of economic events by country. The choice was narrowed to either 1930 or 1931 for each country. Denmark, Finland, France, Netherlands, and Sweden were thought to belong to the 1931 categorization; all other countries of the group belong to the other.

The choice of instruments involves finding those exogenous variables which are closely related to the estimated variables. The instruments are substituted for the endogenous variables by the use of an estimate of the endogenous variables derived from a regression upon the exogenous variables in the equation and the instruments. These instruments are to be related to the endogenous variables and are to be exogenous from the rest of the equation, i.e., uncorrelated with the error term. The exact choice of a method for deter-

7. League (47), vols. 1 and 2.

mining the proper set of instruments is still the subject of an unresolved debate in econometrics. However, the view that the choice of instruments, when limiting their number is necessary, be related to their degree of causality or determinacy of the endogenous variables is accepted as a reasonable criterion. From the viewpoint of this study, that choice will be made from two sets of data. The first set includes commercial policy and income data from countries which have had large trade flow relations with the nation in question. The second set includes crisis date dummies and ROW trade magnitudes.

For example, consider the choice of instruments for equation (17) of the first group country, Belgium. The major decision concerns the choice of another group country whose behavior influences the subject country to a large degree. In the case of Belgium, as with most western nations, the United Kingdom plays that role. Therefore, the instruments for this estimation include commercial policy variables for the United Kingdom along with lagged income for the U.K. In addition, there are two other instruments, an index of world trade and a dummy for 1930. In general, the country choice as to instrument was the United Kingdom for most of western Europe, due to her large influence as the major source of out-of-continent trade, and Germany for eastern Europe. An analysis of the flow percentages of chapter 3 was the major basis for choice.

For the United Kingdom, data on trade with Canada, other Commonwealth countries, and the United States were included as instruments. This approach was in keeping with the concept of the U.K. as a link between the European continent and the rest of the world.

The instrument for world trade activity was the League world quantum of trade index. This is a price-deflated aggregate of world trade reported in League (41) and (47). From the separate sources of this index, I constructed a continuous series, presented in the Appendix. The remaining data were standard League imports and exports along with League and United Nations (42) studies of national income. All of the estimated equations and instruments are presented in the Appendix.

The construction of an appropriate price series was complicated by the fact that there was no way of explicitly identifying the effects of restriction. The data were available for creating a useful series reflecting relative prices. The valuation of each country's exports (exports in home country currency times home country exchange rates) was used to weight the sum of eighteen European export price indices. This weighted sum was converted into an average European external price index. Each individual nation's internal price index was compared to the external index, thereby yielding a goods price index for each country relative to the rest of Europe. This index is a reasonable approximation of a pure relative internal-external price index.

We now have a testable model and appropriate data; what remains is to specify tests and conduct the estimation.

ESTIMATION

The estimation of equation (11) includes the use of an intercept dummy. This specification limits the possible change in the function to a shift with no change in coefficients. An alternative approach was employed which allowed for changes in slope coefficients. Equation (11'), which is equal to (11) without an intercept dummy, was run in three separate versions, (11'a) for dates before the individual country break, (11'b) for dates after the break, and (11'c) for the entire period. Therefore, in equation (11'c) the constraint that $b_{ia} = b_{ib}$ is operative, while in equations (11'a) and (11'b) the constraint is removed. These three equations allow us to conduct a Chow test on the sum of squared residuals; this would indicate whether or not there had been a statistically verifiable change in coefficients across the break.[8]

An alternative approach for determining the possibility of changes in MPM's is employed in the estimation of equation (17) since the validity of a Chow test in a simultaneous setting is unclear. For each national version of equation (17) an additional endogenous variable was added. This variable was the product of the country's income vector (Y_i) and the break date dummy vector. The resulting variable, YD or YDD depending upon the break date, consisted of zero elements up until the break date and values of the income variable thereafter. The coefficients of this variable are equal to the additional change in $b_1'_i$ across the break date. A standard T test determines its significance.

---

8. We are not searching for the break points via an Orcutt grid technique, since we are able to predetermine the break from history and therefore use the information exogenously rather than using the data to discern the dates for us.

Equation (17) was estimated by two-stage least squares with the addition of a Hildreth-Liu autoregressive grid-searching technique. This technique in two-stage least squares requires the use of lagged variables as instruments, an offshoot of the Fair technique for auto-correlation correction of simultaneous equations. Equations (11) and (11'a–c) were estimated using a single-stage Hildreth-Liu for ordinary least squares.

The question of differentiable behavior by subgroups of countries can be considered more rigorously than via a comparison of sub-group propensities or averages alone. Consider the question of the behavior of the industrial versus nonindustrial subgroups. While a comparison of overall propensities offers us certain information, we are provided with no knowledge of the various reactions of subgroups to the depression crisis. The implied question, whether or not reaction to the depression in terms of changes in MPM's differs among subgroups, is answerable by a particular specification of the estimated equations.

Consider taking all of the data relevant to the estimation of the import equations and arranging them in this manner. All of the import data are contained in a single nm × 1 vector where n equals the number of data points and m equals the number of countries; all other data are contained in nm × m matrices whose column vectors contain zero elements everywhere except for right-hand variable data in the same order as the import vector. Expressing the import equation in terms of the variables in their new arrange-ment illustrates that the separate regressions are now collected into a single regression package. The addition of two right-hand variables allows for the testing of hypotheses about differential change in sub-group MPM's over the break period.

$$M = [Y] \, B_1 + [P] \, B_2 + [Z] \, B_3 + \begin{bmatrix} (Y_a) \\ 0 \end{bmatrix} b_{1a}$$

$$+ \begin{bmatrix} 0 \\ (Y_b) \end{bmatrix} b_{1b} \qquad (18)$$

P and Z matrices are constructed from price and all other right-hand variables, respectively, and they are identical in form to the income matrix (Y). An illustrative detail of the income matrix, along with the coefficient change vectors (a) and (b), is reproduced here.

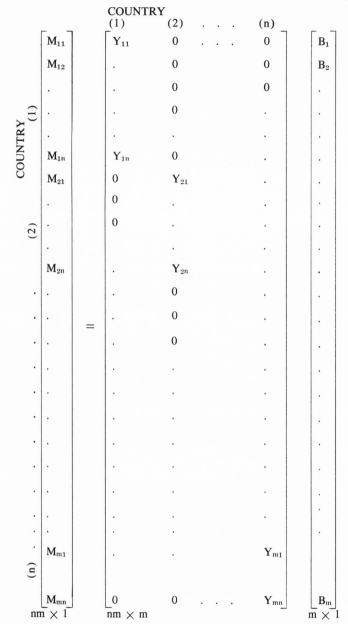

$$
\underset{nm \times 1}{
\begin{matrix}
\text{COUNTRY} \\
\end{matrix}
}
$$

COUNTRY
(1)   (2)   . . .   (n)

$$
\underset{nm \times 1}{
\begin{bmatrix}
M_{11} \\
M_{12} \\
. \\
. \\
. \\
M_{1n} \\
M_{21} \\
. \\
. \\
. \\
M_{2n} \\
. \\
. \\
. \\
. \\
. \\
. \\
. \\
. \\
. \\
M_{m1} \\
M_{mn}
\end{bmatrix}
}
=
\underset{nm \times m}{
\begin{bmatrix}
Y_{11} & 0 & . \,. \,. & 0 \\
. & 0 & & 0 \\
. & 0 & & 0 \\
. & 0 & & \\
. & . & & \\
Y_{1n} & 0 & & \\
0 & Y_{21} & & \\
0 & . & & \\
0 & . & & \\
& . & & \\
. & Y_{2n} & & \\
. & 0 & & \\
. & 0 & & \\
. & 0 & & \\
. & . & & \\
. & . & & \\
. & . & & \\
. & . & & \\
. & . & & \\
. & . & & \\
. & . & & Y_{m1} \\
0 & 0 & . \,. \,. & Y_{mn}
\end{bmatrix}
}
\underset{m \times 1}{
\begin{bmatrix}
B_1 \\
B_2 \\
. \\
. \\
. \\
. \\
. \\
. \\
. \\
. \\
B_m
\end{bmatrix}
}
+
$$

COUNTRY (1) (2) . . . (n)

Equation (18)

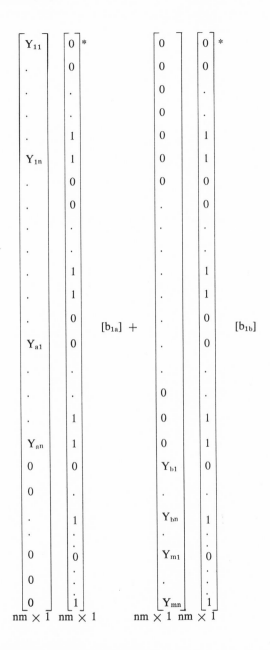

* Multiplication element by element. Each 0/1 vector is a repetition of the break dummy, m times.

The scalar coefficients, b_{1a} and b_{1b}, represent the unconstrained coefficients relevant to a Chow test. The (a) and (b) income vectors are constructed by the addition of the first "a" columns of (Y) which are the income values of the countries in the industrial group. A similar procedure is employed for the nonindustrial (b) group. The two group vectors are multiplied, element by element, by a dummy which has zero for dates before the break and one thereafter for each country's date in turn. The resulting vectors are zero valued for all pre-break dates and Y_i valued for all post-break dates, in addition to being zero valued for all elements of data of countries not within the subgroup.

The implicit assumption of equation (18) is that the change in B_i for group (a) was not equal to the change for group (b). A test of the alternative assumption of an equality of change in the MPM's is provided by the estimation of equation (18′) where $\begin{bmatrix} (Y_a) \\ 0 \end{bmatrix}$ and $\begin{bmatrix} 0 \\ (Y_b) \end{bmatrix}$ are summed to equal $[Y_d]$. $[Y_d]$ is the large equation equivalent of YD in the single equation estimation.

The choice of the division of countries into subgroups will by necessity have arbitrary elements. Two sets of criteria were available, one based upon a division of countries by industrial production, and a second derived from compositional trade flow data. These alternatives lead to different classifications of countries into subgroups. Both sets of subgroups have been tested by the equations.

All of the described equations were estimated, and the resulting output and their implications will now be discussed.

RESULTS

The first and major set of results is the estimates of MPM's from equations (11), (11′c), and (17). These estimates are compared to similar estimates from previous studies (see Table 9).

For the three countries for which there are overlapping estimates (France, Germany, and the United Kingdom) from all three previous works, our best estimate, $b_1′$ of equation (17) by two-stage least squares, is lower than all others for France and Germany and lower than the Neisser and Modigliani estimates for the United Kingdom.

In general, the direction of the difference between my estimates and the estimates of previous works is that mine are lower. Counting all cases where comparisons are possible, equation (17) estimates are lower than the others in twenty-one of twenty-six cases. While this does not prove that the specification used here is correct, over-estimation of the coefficients has the possible implication of simul-taneous equation bias. Johnston (21), in his chapter on simultaneous equation problems, uses the example of a simple consumption and income model in two equations. Consumption is a function of in-

TABLE 9
MARGINAL PROPENSITIES TO IMPORT

	1[a]	2[b]	3[c]	4[d]	5[e]	6[f]
Belgium	0.518	0.500	0.463	—	—	0.63
Bulgaria	0.208	0.168	0.197	—	0.53	—
Czechoslovakia	0.455	0.666	0.568	0.32	0.40	—
Denmark	0.514	0.572	0.577	0.73	0.54	—
Finland	0.363	0.395	0.623	0.93	0.43	—
France	0.175	0.126	0.133	0.25	0.31	0.22[g]
Germany	0.166	0.221	0.252	0.23	0.24	0.37
Great Britain	0.340	0.398	0.396	0.18	0.29	0.42
Hungary	0.326	0.270	0.276	0.37	0.52	—
Netherlands	0.302	0.874	0.901	0.48	—	0.47
Sweden	0.261	0.286	0.334	0.28	0.34	0.41
Switzerland	0.562	0.284	0.265	0.36	0.29	—

a. b_1' of equation (17)
b. b_1' of equation (11)
c. b_1' of equation (11'c)
d. MPM; Polak
e. MPM; Chang
f. MPM; Modigliani & Neisser, from a summation of their separate propensi-ties among various product groups. Belgium and Netherlands estimates were interpolated from their five-country aggregation.
g. French estimates have a downward bias here. The authors did not run esti-mates for all the trade values.

come and income is a function of consumption and other exogenous variables. He proves that an application of least squares to the consumption function, even when problems of heteroscedasticity, autocorrelation, and sample size are removed, will produce estimates of the MPC which are upward biased. My simultaneous model of import functions is analogous to the simple model in Johnston's exposition. By failing to measure the interrelatedness of countries' import functions and by omitting commercial policy vectors, the previous studies have overestimated the MPM's.

The slopes in equation (11) are generally lower than those esti-mated by equation (11'c). The only difference between the estimates is the addition in (11) of a break-date dummy. The first test of the significance of the break dates was successful. The effect of the break upon slope changes will be considered later.

The income coefficients of equation (17), along with tariff level data mentioned, provide us with the information necessary to calculate the foreign trade multipliers: m_T, no expenditure change from tariff revenue (see Table 10), and m_T^f, full expenditure change (see Table 11). Included in Table 10 is a listing of Polak's multipliers

TABLE 10
TRADE-INCOME EFFECTS, NONEXPENDITURE CHANGE MULTIPLIERS

	(m_0)[a]	(m_p)[b]	(m_1)[c]	(m_2)[d]	(m_3)[e]
Belgium	1.543	—	—	1.613	1.845
Bulgaria	2.959	—	—	3.164	3.682
Czechoslovakia	1.709	2.55	—	1.894	2.572
Denmark	1.553	1.20	1.591	—	—
Finland	2.028	1.34	—	2.195	2.403
France	3.279	1.12	—	3.353	4.730
Germany	3.378	2.48	—	3.442	4.843
Hungary	2.193	1.80	—	2.366	2.375
Netherlands	2.315	1.60	2.334	—	—
Sweden	2.558	2.53	—	2.646	2.704
Switzerland	1.450	1.55	—	1.553	1.585
United Kingdom	2.128	—	2.149	—	2.325

NOTE: All internal MPM's from two-stage estimation of equation (17) for each country. Retained revenue from $b_1'T_i$ yields no change in total expenditure.
a. m_0: T = 0
b. m_p: T = 0, Polak's estimates
c. m_1: T = 1925
d. m_2: T = 1927
e. m_3: T = 1931

(m_p) and my calculated values of a free-trade multiplier (m_0) for comparison. Polak's multipliers were calculated without consideration of the effects of tariffs. The (m_0) estimates serve as the lower bound of the general level of the impact of trade upon income. The (m_0)'s range from 1.450 for Switzerland to 3.378 for Germany; the mean value of 2.4 exceeds the Polak average of 1.8.

In addition to an interest in the levels of calculated multipliers, there are various implications to be garnered from a comparison of multipliers, both over time, reflecting changes in tariff levels, and between multipliers, representing the effects of different assumptions about tariff-revenue expenditure. Further comparisons of multiplier levels are made between average levels of various national

TABLE 11
TRADE-INCOME EFFECTS, FULL EXPENDITURE CHANGE MULTIPLIERS

	(m_1^f)	(m_2^f)	(m_3^f)
Belgium		1.702	1.984
Bulgaria		3.497	4.182
Czechoslovakia		2.129	2.902
Denmark	1.638		
Finland		2.421	2.734
France		3.484 ·	4.877
Germany		3.555	6.994
Hungary		2.608	2.687
Netherlands	2.442		
Sweden		2.777	2.884
Switzerland		1.687	1.756
United Kingdom	2.178		2.475

NOTE: $m_0^f = m_0$ Table; $m_{1,2,3} = T = 1925, 1927, 1931$. All internal MPM's from two-stage estimation of equation (17) for each country. Retained revenue from $b_1'T_1 = $ change in expenditure.

subgroups. Therefore, the possible range (in a statistical sense) of our calculated multiplier values is necessary information for interpretation of multiplier levels and differentials.

Table 12 presents minimum and maximum values of the calculated multipliers, m_T and m_T^f, at a confidence level of 90 per cent for 1931 tariff rate values. Since the tariff rates are nonstochastic, all multipliers calculated under the same retention assumption will

TABLE 12
MINIMUM AND MAXIMUM MULTIPLIERS

	m_{Tmax}	m_{Tmin}	$m_T^f{}_{max}$	$m_T^f{}_{min}$
Belgium	1.920	1.465	2.058	1.613
Bulgaria	3.588	3.060	4.098	3.639
Czechoslovakia	2.283	1.787	2.632	2.168
Denmark[a]	1.759	1.453	1.805	1.502
Finland	2.841	1.928	3.145	2.289
France	4.299	3.165	4.467	3.432
Germany	4.463	2.913	4.633	3.166
Hungary	3.911	1.817	4.132	2.162
Netherlands[a]	3.312	1.807	3.335	1.837
Sweden	2.870	2.518	3.044	2.705
Switzerland	2.043	1.310	2.202	1.490
United Kingdom	2.716	1.913	2.855	2.074

NOTE: Confidence limits were calculated at the 10 per cent level; tariff rates for multipliers are from 1931.
a. Tariff rates used are from 1925.

have identical statistical properties except for scale. The postdepression, 1931 tariff rate multipliers have the widest absolute variation, and therefore these extreme values include within their bounds all of the other multiplier values. The minimum and maximum values of the multipliers were calculated by successive generation of individual multipliers using slope coefficients to derive an upper and lower estimate term (k). For each individual country, multipliers were calculated using a corrected MPM value of $b_1'^*$

$$b_1'^* = b_1' \pm k \tag{19}$$

where $k = t_{0.10[n-2]} \times \hat{\sigma}_{b_1}$.

In the cases where tariff level data were not available for 1931 (Denmark and Netherlands), 1925 data were used.

As expected, there is variation in the size of the individual ranges, reflecting variations in the fitting of the equations. In spite of this, the minimum values indicate that there was a substantial income reaction to trade changes. The vulnerability of income to trade destruction is apparent.

Though no period in twentieth-century Europe can be said to have been dominated by free trade, an examination of the differences in the impact of trade upon income between a zero tariff base and a predepression protectionist level is interesting. On average the imposition of tariffs increases the trade multiplier by an amount equal to 10 per cent of income.

The subgroup divisions are also revealing (see Table 13). The combination of higher MPM's and higher predepression tariffs results in a protection versus free trade multiplier differential which is almost 2.25 times as great for eastern Europe as it is for western Europe. A similar result is found for a division of protection versus free trade differentials by industrial and nonindustrial subgroups, with the differential being twice as large for nonindustrial nations. Because eastern and nonindustrial nations were more prone to protection, their incomes were more prone to variation from trade loss. This conclusion must be qualified by the fact of a much larger range of possible multiplier values, within the same confidence limits, for eastern and nonindustrial countries.

A comparison of the change in multiplier values across the depression crisis will generate a measure of the additional losses from restriction and trade destruction which were suffered after the onset of the depression. The overall multiplier increase from predepression to postdepression exceeds the comparative differential from free trade to predepression levels by more than five times. For the more trade-dependent NICE countries, the comparative change in multipliers is even larger. The increases in income loss for a given loss in trade approach 50 per cent of income over the depression.

TABLE 13
MULTIPLIER DIFFERENTIALS

| | (Tariff level) Changes | | (Revenue-retention) Assumption changes | |
	$(m_2 - m_0)$	$(m_3 - m_2)$	$(m_2^f - m_2)$	$(m_3^f - m_3)$
Overall				
average	0.096	0.512	0.148	0.435
East	0.156	0.651	0.231	0.823
West	0.066	0.417	0.107	0.177
Industrial	0.072	0.625	0.012	0.444
Nonindustrial	0.145	0.245	0.212	0.383

NOTE: m_1 substituted for m_2 where m_2 data are missing.

The first two sets of multiplier differentials (Table 13) represented changes in multiplier values because of changes of tariff levels within two time periods. The second two sets of differentials represent the gains in multiplier values which would occur when the assumption of zero expenditure of tariff revenues was changed to an assumption of full expenditure, also for two separate time periods. While the question of the correct assumption has differing implications before and after the depression, we can investigate as a single question which assumption is more empirically valid.

It is impossible to trace the effect of any given governmental receipt upon the expenditures for a nation. We must infer, from available data and policy, whether an assumption about the effects of increased revenues upon expenditure is consistent with the general fiscal policy of a country. We have two basic sources of relevant information, the percentage of revenue which customs receipts represented and the size of budgetary surpluses or deficits. Both types of data are available for only a few years during the period and for less than all of our group countries.[9] All of the available statistics have been compiled and presented in Tables 14 and 15.

9. League (47), 1:269, 2:163–64, and 3:175.

TABLE 14
CUSTOMS RECEIPTS AS A PERCENTAGE OF TAX REVENUES

	1927	1929	1934
Belgium	11.0	13.1	17.7
Bulgaria	30.0	30.2	19.7
Czechoslovakia	13.0		
Denmark	25.0	26.4	23.6
Finland	57.0	57.2	57.3
France	6.0	9.4	12.2
Germany		18.3	21.8
Hungary		15.0	5.2
Netherlands	11.0	11.9	22.2
Sweden	25.0	26.9	19.3
Switzerland	68.0	72.5	75.9
United Kingdom	16.0	18.3	27.5

Customs receipts represent a sizable portion of revenue for most countries. For a majority of countries this proportion grew between 1927 and 1929 (all nine of the countries for which data exist) and between 1929 and 1934 (seven out of eleven show a higher proportion and one other had a slight decline). The growth in the percentage of custom receipts in national budgets is especially startling

TABLE 15
BUDGETARY SURPLUS (+) OR DEFICIT (−)

	1929	1931	1933	1937
Belgium	+1315		− 846	− 2608
	(9.6)		(8.2)	(24.3)
Czechoslovakia	+ 169	−3128		
	(2.0)	(34.0)		
France[a]	+3929	−5484	−11509	−21436
	(8.2)	(11.4)	(26.5)	(48.7)
Germany	− 712	− 602	− 257	
	(7.0)	(7.0)	(4.3)	
Hungary	− 31		− 66	− 12
	(2.1)		(5.9)	(0.9)
Netherlands	− 47	− 146		
	(5.0)	(21.0)		
Sweden	− 29	− 116	− 146	+ 90
	(4.0)	(15.0)	(18.4)	(6.7)
Switzerland		+ 2	− 74	− 16
		(1.0)	(16.2)	(2.9)
United Kingdom	− 25	− 8	+ 39	− 25
	(3.0)	(1.0)	(4.8)	(2.6)

NOTE: ( ) Percentage of total receipts. All values are (000,000) of own country currency.
a. 1928 data

in the latter period for which there was a substantial fall in prices and trade. Customs receipts appear to have been a more stable part of revenue than alternative sources. Condliffe, writing in the League's *World Economic Survey 1933–34*, noted that "The importance of customs duties in almost every budget is due not only to the aggregate of revenue so collected, but to its elasticity. . . . Additional duties upon imports have always been one of the first lines of reserve upon which Ministers of Finance may call in an emergency."

Having established the importance of customs duties in revenue, we must also show that all of the revenue collected would have been spent. Of the three possible conditions of a national budget, surplus, balanced, or deficit, only the first could be associated with a fiscal policy in which tariff revenue was not spent. Moreover, even when there exists a surplus budget, if the surplus declines over time (i.e., the budget is becoming expansionary), the assumption of expenditure of a large portion, if not all, of tariff revenues is tenable. Table 15 indicates that for the second half of the interwar period the full expenditure of tariff revenue assumption is preferable in light of the expansionary nature of national budgets.

During the interwar period, the dominant fiscal philosophy was the pursuance of balanced budgets. During the predepression period we can only rely upon that philosophy for our inference that all tariff revenues were spent. During the postdepression period, when budgets were generally in deficit while the balanced budget ideology remained, we can be sure that there were no tariff revenue funds which were not expended. This analysis argues strongly that the larger ($m_T{}^f$) multiplier was appropriate as an estimate of the trade loss effect upon income.

The method which was used for testing the effect of the break date upon import propensities was different for the single equation and simultaneous equation estimations. For the ordinary least squares equations, a Chow test was employed for equations (11'a), (11'b), and (11'c). The MPM's before and after the break, for each individual country, and the appropriate test statistics are presented in Table 16, along with the change and percentage change in the coefficients. The F statistic rejecting the hypothesis that the MPM's were the same throughout the period was significant in all but three cases. Two of the three countries for which the Chow test failed exhibited positive changes in their MPM's, which would have been counterintuitive had the tests been significant.

TABLE 16

CHANGES IN THE MARGINAL PROPENSITIES TO IMPORT:

OLSQ ESTIMATES FROM EQUATIONS 11'a, 11'b, AND 11'c

	Early MPM	Late MPM	± Δ	%Δ ±	F(3,8)	Level
Belgium	.428	.508	+.080	+18.5	7.18	0.010
Bulgaria	.379	.191	−.188	−49.4	3.83	0.100
Czechoslovakia	.348	.312	−.036	−10.3	2.60	0.150
Denmark	.578	.437	−.141	−32.7	11.99	0.150
Finland	.836	.466	−.430	−51.5	14.40	0.010
France	.080	.018	−.062	−77.6	18.30	0.010
Germany	.539	.053	−.486	−90.2	13.51	0.010
Hungary	.408	.119	−.289	−70.9	6.64	0.025
Netherlands	.523	.959	+.436	+83.3	3.28	0.100
Sweden	.348	.266	−.082	−23.4	9.88	0.010
Switzerland	.263	.458	+.195	+14.4	0.88	N.S.
United Kingdom	.296	.221	−.075	−25.5	3.46	0.010

NOTE: For the Chow test: $\dfrac{Q_1 - Q_2/k}{Q_2/T - 2k}$; k = 3; T = 14.

The test for changes in the MPM's within a simultaneous setting involved the addition of the aforementioned YD or YDD variable. The coefficient of YD/YDD was significantly less than zero in seven cases and negative in ten (see Table 17). The magnitudes of the changes in MPM were essentially the same in both versions of the estimation.

TABLE 17

CHANGES IN THE MARGINAL PROPENSITIES TO IMPORT:

TSLQ ESTIMATES FROM EQUATION (17)

	Early MPM	Late MPM	± Δ	± % Δ	T stat.
Belgium	.518	.446	−.072	−13.9	−1.46
Bulgaria	.208	.164	−.042	−20.2	−3.81
Czechoslovakia	.455	.297	−.158	−34.7	−2.11
Denmark	.514	.218	−.296	−57.5	−2.21
Finland	.363	.332	−.031	− 8.5	−0.22
France	.175	.084	−.091	−52.0	−4.36
Germany	.166	.079	−.087	−52.4	−4.84
Hungary	.326	.335	+.009	+ 2.3	+0.18
Netherlands	.302	.725	+.423	+140	+1.70
Sweden	.261	.257	−.004	− 1.5	−0.24
Switzerland	.562	.435	−.127	−22.5	−0.52
United Kingdom	.340	.321	−.019	− 5.6	−1.60

NOTE: T test on $b_{D, DD}$ coefficient in equation (17).

These results provide strong confirmation that a possible source of change in the trade and income relationship, namely a lowering of import propensities, did in fact occur. This lowering of MPM's had the effect of causing the impact of trade destruction upon income to be greater than would be indicated by either standard models of fixed import propensities or by previous studies. Not only did the break date cause a sharp reduction in trade and income but the shape of the relationship appears to have been altered.

The large percentage changes in MPM's for France and Germany in both sets of tests are suggestive of a possible interpretation of the propensity change. Both Germany and France had a strong national policy of trade isolation, especially in the latter part of the period. We can explain the change in MPM's by an appeal to non-economic considerations, namely that the taste for foreign products changed across the break. This interpretation implies that there may have been a nationalistic or chauvinistic retreat from trade. This activity may have included some policies and taste changes which were retaliatory in nature. Moreover, we cannot infer that the change in MPM's represents the absence of nontariff barriers in estimation since these were included in the set of exogenous variables used in the estimation of equation (17). We can also dismiss the possibility that the change in MPM's is the result of an error in b_1' estimation due to the misspecification of the role of tariffs in the import function. As mentioned, the bias in the coefficients introduced by this error would be in an upward direction and therefore could not account for the downward change which was observed.[10]

The large regression equations (18) and (18') were run to test the existence of differential MPM changes for industrial and non-industrial subgroups. The regressions have indicated that the industrial subgroup experienced changes in its MPM's which were greater than the changes experienced by the nonindustrial subgroup.

There were two possible categorizations of our group countries into industrial subgroups. When the grouping was determined by industrial production, the relevant F statistic for the test that $b_{1a} \neq b_{1b}$ was equal to 3.705 (5 per cent level). The same test for a subgrouping determined by trade flows produced an F statistic of 3.915 (10 per cent). The changes in the average coefficient for each subgroup were as follows:

10. See footnote 3.

Subgrouping criteria	Change in b_{1a}	Change in b_{1b}
Industrial production	$-.127$	$-.029$
Trade flows	$-.157$	$-.035$

Both sets of subgroups produced a passing F statistic with respect to differential change. As the results show, the change in MPM's for subgroup a, industrial countries, was much larger than for the b group. In addition, the significance levels of the income coefficients were much higher for the a group. The implication is that, although the NICE countries were more susceptible to trade-induced income changes via the multiplier, the disaggregation by productive activity indicates that the ICE nations may have had strong income elasticity effects. These effects reduced the ICE countries' trade functions in the presence of falling income.

The statistical results from the inclusion of price variables are disappointing. Price variables were less than completely effective in improving estimations of ordinary least squares equations in their role as explanatory variables, nor were they completely effective in estimations of two-stage least squares in their role as endogenous variables. An inherent weakness of the price series was the absence of explicit information as to the influence of policy and restrictions upon national price levels. These problems notwithstanding, the price variable performance was acceptable in a majority of cases. The expected positive sign occurs in half of the estimates of equation (11) and in slightly more than half of the estimates of equation (17). Price variables were significant nine times in the equation (11) estimates and eight times in the equation (17) runs.

The presence of negative price coefficients could be explained by a variety of possible conditions. Instability, inferiority, and/or multiple equilibria could all account for the observation of wrong signed coefficients. However, the realistic admission that the data were weak in their ability to capture all of the relevant information is just as sufficient an explanation. These less-than-perfect price results are, nevertheless, superior to those produced in the cited Polak study. Polak's specifications produced only three out of fourteen cases of measurable price effects, while this study counts sixteen out of twenty-four.

Although traditional trade theory is only concerned with relative price change, the declining level of absolute prices should be of interest. Overall European prices fell by 11.8 per cent from 1929 to 1930 and by an additional 12.0 per cent from 1930 to 1931. I will not argue strongly in favor of Pigou or real balance effects as powerful economic variables; however, some of the reversal of import price relations could have been due, in part, to price-induced income changes. The impact of price on income via trade was possibly more powerful than the data indicated. The decline in prices was deep and sustained. The general price level in Europe did not return to its predepression level until World War II.

These price effects notwithstanding, the conclusion to this point must be that the effects of trade upon income were sizable and varied.

We have only to consider a final body of estimated and generated values to conclude the investigation. The commercial policy variables will be discussed in the section dealing with policy. We will attempt to ascertain the role of policy changes in two distinct ways. The first approach will follow the lines which have been used up to this point, namely an analysis of the implications of the coefficients estimated for commercial policy variables. The second approach will involve our discussion of the probable effects which would have come about had policy restrictions not been enforced as they were during the interwar period. This approach will be facilitated by the use of generated values of national incomes, under alternative states of nature, which are implied by the estimated simultaneous model.

COMMERCIAL POLICY VARIABLES AND GENERATED INCOME COMPARISONS

Commercial policy information, used as data, was entered into the estimation procedure in four ways: as an exchange rate-cum-devaluation index (EX), as a subjective tariff and nontariff restriction level ranking (TI and TII), as instruments for "other country" estimations of equation (17), and as computed tariff rate levels for use in the generation of foreign trade multipliers (m_T and $m_T{}^f$).

EX as an exogenous variable produced six positive and five negative coefficients, six of which were significant. The expected positive relationship in the import function is only weakly indicated. Devaluations during recovery in the latter part of the period may have obscured the relationships.

The performance of the ranked variables was moderately successful. There were seven negative coefficients associated with the second rank (TI) and nine negative values for the third (TII). These coefficients were significant in seven and six cases, respectively.

While the rankings were subjective and qualitative, so that the absolute sizes of the coefficients are not useful for interpretation, there are implications to be gained from an inspection of the relative sizes of the coefficients of the two explicit rank variables. We would expect the coefficients of TII to exceed those of TI, since TII represents a more intense level of home country import restriction. TII was larger than TI (more negative) in nine out of twelve instances. The general result of negative coefficients was not the result of a reflection of the same information which caused the dummy variables to exhibit negative values since the rankings were neither uniform nor confined to the break period.

The tariff level data are, of course, underestimates of the total restrictionist activity. Even these lower bound values exhibit considerable impact upon the trade and income relationship. The marginal income effect of tariff level changes reaches almost 50 per cent of the change in income when calculated from foreign trade multipliers. The tariff level data themselves show large gains ranging between 50 and 100 per cent in the overall rate between 1927 and 1931.

The use of policy variables as instruments is a technique which, by its nature, is not subject to tests of the effectiveness of the procedure, since we are using these variables as instruments for a priori reasons. To the extent that estimates resulting from equation (17) are an improvement over previous estimates and our own equation (11) results, the use of external policy variables as instruments deserves part of the credit for that improvement.

In retrospect, history tells more about commercial policy than does the output of estimation techniques which employ the historical information. Nevertheless, as a general statement, the fact that restrictionist policies reduced trade is unquestionable. We have also established via the construction of appropriate multipliers, and previously by the calculation of gross measures of income loss from trade, that trade losses contributed to a decline in income.

By the establishment of a relationship between policy and trade and, further, by the establishment of a relationship between trade and income, it would be a simple matter to infer the existence of a relationship between reductions in income and changes in policy. The quality of the results garnered from the inclusion of policy variables is such that further demonstration of the relationship between policy and income appears necessary. We require more than the establishment of policy data as significant variables in a trade and income model.

Considering the trade and income model as a whole, we can bypass the two-step relationship of policy with trade and then trade with income and pose this question: How much would income have changed if the restrictionist policies were not pursued? The answer would demonstrate, in terms of income levels directly, the extent of the impact of policy upon income.

We already know that the process of income loss from policy is transmitted via trade losses; therefore, the generated values of income decline could be inferred to equal the loss in income resulting from trade destruction which in turn was the result of changes in policy. We must qualify our interpretations, since not all of the loss of trade resulted from policy changes. There were reductions in trade propensities which were the result of other factors (possibly tastes). We will consider this last point next, when we generate the alternative income values.

The technique of generating alternative income values involves the use of the estimated coefficients of the simultaneous model to simulate income values, over our research period, which the model generates under changed assumptions. These changed assumptions are introduced to the model by varying the actual values of exogenous variables. For several reasons the period of the simulation will be limited from the break date until 1936. The quality of the estimated values of the model, in terms of goodness of fit, is superior inside the time range of the estimation. Also, our major interest in policy changes occurs after the depression break date in most countries. The generation of alternative income values will begin in the break-date year via a complete or partial change in the actual value of certain exogenous variables. The most important use of the output of the simulation will be in the comparison of income values under alternative contrafactual realities.

This process of comparison leads us to the question of a bench mark for the state of nature in which all the exogenous activity was represented by the actual values recorded. The obvious choice of actual income as the set of values with which to compare changed income series is not the optimal choice. As with any statistical model, there is a portion of the difference between actual income levels and the levels implied by the model which are due to statistical error terms and random variations. If we were to compare the changed income series with the actual income series, part of the difference observed would be attributable to statistical noise. This condition would be tolerable if we could assign a value to the part of the observed differences which results from noise and the part that results from changed exogenous variables, but that assignation is impossible. Therefore, we need another income series for each country, one which will have all of the same conditions of exogenous variables as those in actual income, but the statistical properties of the series are to be the same as for the alternative income series. The set of income values which possesses such properties is the generated value of income with no changes in exogenous variables $(\hat{Y})$.

The three alternative series which will be compared to $\hat{Y}$ represent alternative states of nature. The first series is that of income values which are generated by the model with a constructed set of policy variables. This set is equal to the actual level of policy variables up to the break date. In this alternative, policy did not change but all other exogenous variables did. The resulting income series $(\hat{Y}_1)$ will reflect the alternative values of income which result from an abstinence of policy change. The difference between $\hat{Y}_1$ and $\hat{Y}$ for any nation is the gain in income from the implementation of a predepression policy. Conversely, $\hat{Y}_1 - \hat{Y}$ equals the loss of income as a result of the actual restrictionist commercial policy.

The second income series results from the income values generated when there is no change in MPM's over the break date. Taking, as we did earlier, the changes in MPM to reflect changes in the national taste for traded goods, we can infer that an income stream which was generated by the model when there was no change in MPM's $(\hat{Y}_2)$ reflects changes in income which would have occurred had there been no change in taste vis-à-vis trade goods. The difference, $\hat{Y}_2 - \hat{Y}$, would equal the loss in income sustained because of the change in tastes.

The last alternative income series is the result of combining the assumptions of $\hat{Y}_1$ and $\hat{Y}_2$. $\hat{Y}_3$ equals the income stream generated when all exogenous variables remained at their pre-break level. The values of the generated $(\hat{Y})$s, $\hat{Y}$ differentials, and relevant percentage changes $(\bar{Y})$s are reproduced in the appendix.

I have transferred the percentage changes in alternative income streams for three countries into graphical form (see Figs. 4–6). The contrafactual results for France and Germany are closer to each other than the results for the United Kingdom. These two major ICE nations both exhibit large overall effects, the maximum peaking over 100 per cent. The peak occurs at an earlier date for Germany (1932) than for France (1934). For both nations, taste has an effect which is slightly stronger than policy except for the period immediately following the break. These results are reconcilable with history. French isolation from trade was so severe that the probable benefits to her income, had her policies and tastes been different, stretch out for the longest period of time among the major countries. The lower effects of policy and taste change for Germany after 1932 probably reflect her aggressive commercial activity outside of western Europe.

In Figure 6, it can be seen that the alternative experience of the United Kingdom was very different from the countries on the continent. The level of income loss inferred from taste and policy change is considerably lower, only slightly exceeding 30 per cent at its peak in 1933. Moreover, for the United Kingdom, taste effects were much lower than policy effects. The relative position of taste and policy effects in the U.K. is the reverse of their positions for France and Germany. This fact reflects the greater force of nationalistic protectionism on the continent. While the U.K. undertook severe changes in commercial policy, she did not experience changes in the taste patterns for goods to the same degree as on the continent.

In all three countries there were dates for which the total percentage differential was less than one or both of the separate differentials. This can only be explained by the existence of some negative interaction between changes in policy and changes in taste. Moreover, the percentage income change resulting from the total effect is less than the sum of the effects resulting from policy and taste alterations. This is true for every simulation. The possibility of a negative relationship between taste and policy must be assumed to be extremely large in order to account for this sizable loss in total effect.

Changes in MPM's may have been influenced by price changes in a manner which was not specified. If so, policy actions which increase the effective prices of imports would result in MPM changes which move in the opposite direction.

We cannot dismiss the possibility that the phenomenon of a

lessened total effect is the result of an overlapping of the separate policy and taste effects. This possibility would effect the size of the implied taste and/or total effects, but not the policy effects. This is true because the specification of taste changes, as a shift in MPM's, is more likely to have included some policy variable effects rather than vice versa.

On Table 18, and Figures 7 and 8, I have attempted to generalize the separate alternative income streams for each nation. All of the data in the table represent mean values of percentage differentials weighted by income levels. The peak values of approximately 60 per cent represent the best estimate of the effect upon income from policy changes, allowing for some time (three to four years) to pass. The initial year value of some 22 per cent would be the short-run impact of policy change upon income.

A disaggregation of the group data into ICE and NICE countries reveals some interesting differences. Except for a period just following the change in policy, the policy impact upon income is larger for ICE nations than for NICE. This result is dominated by the perversity of taste effects being larger than all effects throughout the period for NICE nations. Perhaps because of the greater level of trade interconnection among ICE countries, we observe that the impact upon income is larger for the NICE nation initially, as expected, but the interconnections cause the ICE impact to continue to rise, while NICE countries show a leveling off of the impact of policy and taste effects.

The direct impact of policy upon income produces results which are similar to implications garnered from considering the policy and trade and then trade and income relationships.

TABLE 18
Mean Percentage Change over Estimated Incomes

	GROUP			ICE			NICE		
	$\tilde{\tilde{Y}}_1$[a]	$\tilde{\tilde{Y}}_2$[b]	$\tilde{\tilde{Y}}_3$[c]	$\tilde{\tilde{Y}}_1$	$\tilde{\tilde{Y}}_2$	$\tilde{\tilde{Y}}_3$	$\tilde{\tilde{Y}}_1$	$\tilde{\tilde{Y}}_2$	$\tilde{\tilde{Y}}_3$
1930[d]	22.5	16.3	23.7	21.2	11.1	22.2	29.6	33.0	31.8
1931	31.4	30.5	32.3	35.0	30.3	35.8	27.6	35.0	28.8
1932	59.6	58.8	62.3	70.5	66.9	73.5	47.9	53.1	50.4
1933	59.5	62.0	61.4	66.4	66.9	68.2	54.4	62.6	56.9
1934	55.5	63.1	63.3	75.7	73.9	76.3	49.4	55.2	50.4
1935	57.9	57.8	57.8	73.6	72.0	73.5	41.0	43.1	41.1
1936	47.1	44.9	46.0	58.6	53.7	56.4	36.4	38.5	37.0

a. $\tilde{\tilde{Y}}_1 = \Sigma \dfrac{\hat{Y}_1 - \hat{Y}}{\hat{Y}}$ %; policy effect on income.

b. $\tilde{\tilde{Y}}_2 = \Sigma \dfrac{\hat{Y}_2 - \hat{Y}}{\hat{Y}}$ %; taste effect on income.

c. $\tilde{\tilde{Y}}_3 = \Sigma \dfrac{\hat{Y}_3 - \hat{Y}}{\hat{Y}}$ %; total trade effect on income.

d. For CDD countries only.

Σ = Over group and subgroup countries.

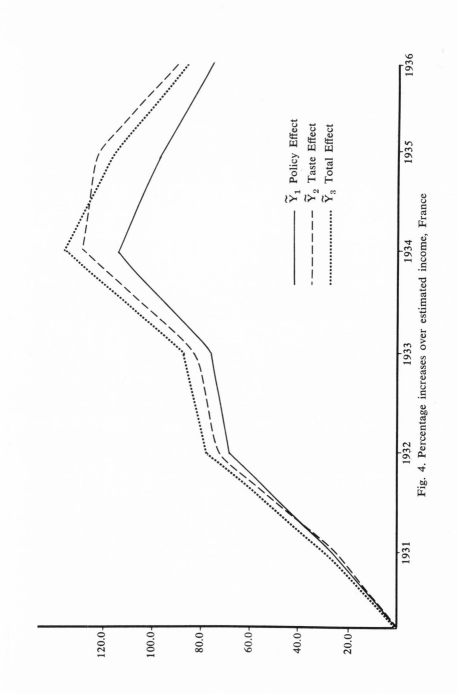

Fig. 4. Percentage increases over estimated income, France

$\tilde{Y}_1$ Policy Effect
$\tilde{Y}_2$ Taste Effect
$\tilde{Y}_3$ Total Effect

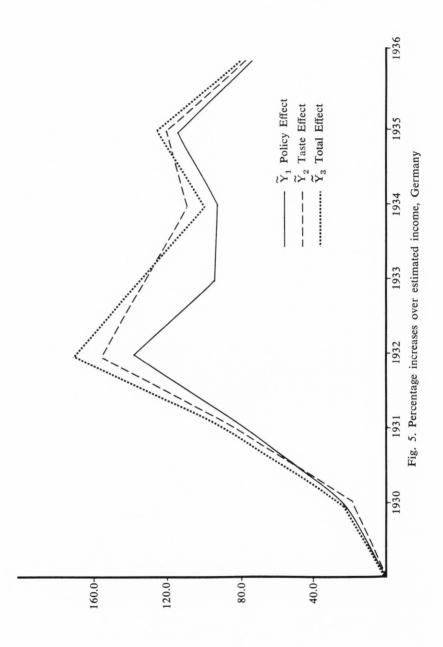

Fig. 5. Percentage increases over estimated income, Germany

$\tilde{Y}_1$ Policy Effect
$\tilde{Y}_2$ Taste Effect
$\tilde{Y}_3$ Total Effect

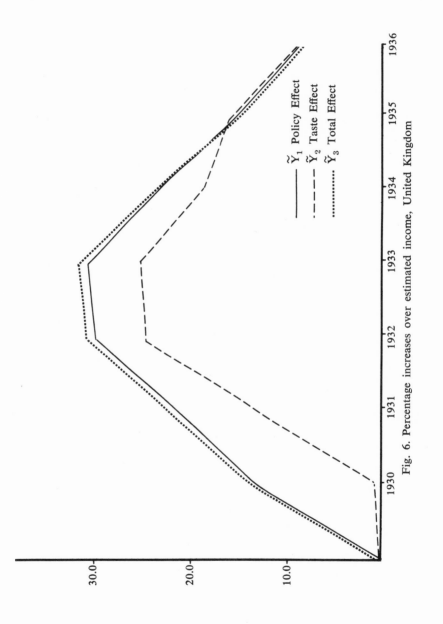

Fig. 6. Percentage increases over estimated income, United Kingdom

$\tilde{Y}_1$ Policy Effect
$\tilde{Y}_2$ Taste Effect
$\tilde{Y}_3$ Total Effect

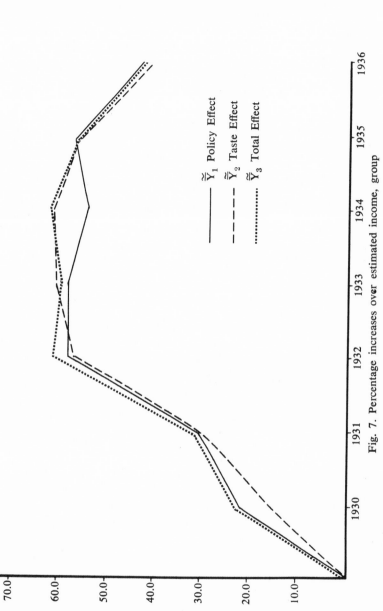

Fig. 7. Percentage increases over estimated income, group

$\widetilde{\widetilde{Y}}_1$ Policy Effect

$\widetilde{\widetilde{Y}}_2$ Taste Effect

$\widetilde{\widetilde{Y}}_3$ Total Effect

70.0

60.0

50.0

40.0

30.0

20.0

10.0

1930   1931   1932   1933   1934   1935   1936

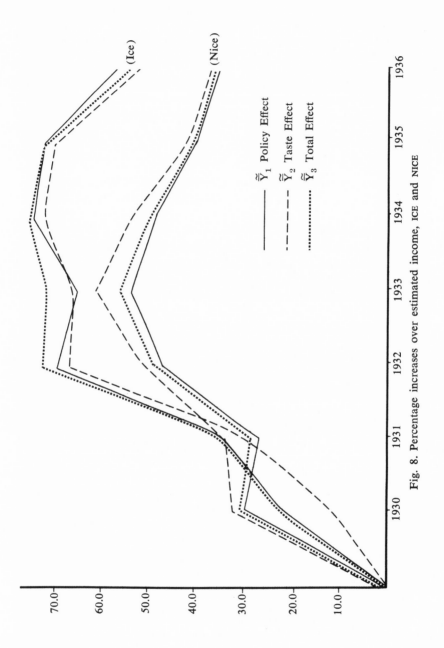

Fig. 8. Percentage increases over estimated income, ICE and NICE

$\tilde{\tilde{Y}}_1$ Policy Effect
$\tilde{Y}_2$ Taste Effect
$\tilde{Y}_3$ Total Effect

5

A Synthesis of Policy Implications

SEVERAL FACTS have emerged from the study, and the questions posed at the onset of the work have been answered, in part. The measurement of the extent of the trade and income relationship points to sizable income reactions to the loss of trade over the interwar period.

The question of the interaction upon income and trade policy was answered in stages from the three major divisions of the work. The commercial policy history points rather sharply to a pattern of reaction to British and world economic conditions and policies which initiated a massive movement toward the restriction of trade. The entire postwar history was one of hesitant recovery in policy which was abandoned at the first sign of crisis. The propensity to turn to the destructive regulation of trade when individual positions were threatened had the inevitable result of contracting total trade because of the tightly closed trade relationship of the European economy.

We also inspected the reactions of trade to policy by an analysis of the flow patterns of trade inside and outside of Europe. Here, too, commercial policy seems to have reduced the trading level in all cases. The final introduction of policy measures into the econometric model illuminated the crucial role of policy in the general model. Conceptually, policy held the role of tying the system together and was the primary force which drove the mechanism of change in the relationships.

The specification of a changing MPM over the break period seems to have improved on previous models. The massive reductions in all countries' incomes which led to general trade loss and protectionist trade destruction were generated via the import and income relationship and by a coincidental change in that relationship. The

105

presumption that import propensities which change over the period should be interpreted as changes in taste is consistent with history and with the specification of the model which includes trade restriction variables explicitly.

The attempt to quantify the loss of income due to trade destruction has taken three distinct forms, gross measures of the impact of trade upon income, construction of foreign trade multipliers, and differentials in generated values of income under alternative assumptions. The combination of these measures produces an overall picture of the trade and income relationship. Moreover, the diverse measures are compatible in that they yield values which can be reconciled. The gross measure of trade activity relative to income is approximately 20 per cent for the entire period and is almost equal to the average value of 22 per cent for the total first-year impact of policy change in the value of the generated income differential. The gross trade activity measure is a year-for-year quantity; therefore, its value is compatible with the short-run generated value.

Multipliers are estimates of the changes in income which are the result of an exogenous change. Therefore, multipliers predict the level of the new equilibrium which comes about after the passage of time, i.e., the long-run effects of trade destruction. The average multiplier value of 2.9 for the full expenditure $(m_T{}^f)$ case for all group countries is not dissimilar to the mean value of 2.6 for cumulated income differentials from policy change over the estimated period.

The assumption that there would have been no other factors affecting the model after the break, in the context of assuming that policy and tastes were unchanged, is untenable. Therefore, the short-run effects are probably closer to the "true" value of the loss of income which resulted as a direct consequence of trade destruction.

The disaggregation of nations into subgroups was most successful in separating out the behavioral differences of eastern and western European countries. This was especially true of trade flows and the ascendancy of "new" German policies in the east. Moreover, the disaggregation produced significant estimation of the differences among ICE and NICE nations.

In general, the reactions to the swift turn of events occurring during the break period were manifested as greater changes in all measures than the changes which occurred during any other period. Restrictions, propensities, prices, and so on, all combined to present a picture of a severe reaction, manifested through policy actions, to the events of the 1930–31 period.

A combination of the three major sections of the work suggests a mosaic of a Europe ripe for collapse. The inherent debt structure after the war, hyperinflated currencies, the political and economic implications of Versailles, the legacy of wartime restrictions, and other conditions all combined with the high degree of economic interdependence via trade to create a domino structure. I have concentrated on British policies and the financial crisis as the initiating causes of the retaliation which marked the fall of the structure of international commerce. This identification of an initiating cause for retaliation is not as important as the recognition of the structure itself. Almost any shock would have initiated the contracting retaliatory process; knowing which shock was the culprit is less important than knowing that there was a culprit at all.

Some obvious questions have not been raised. These questions are concerned with the relationship of the trade structure to the length and depth of the depression. The question of why the depression had been as severe as it was has been of major interest to economists. At this point, I can only offer the conjecture that nonmarket aspects of restrictionist warfare introduced an element of intransigence into economic relationships. Kindleberger speaks of national pride and commercial policy as causing nations to incur costs which are not explicit to the policy-makers. The length of the depression may have been influenced by the presence of trade restrictions as a major factor in the decline, restrictions being essentially asymmetric in terms of their likelihood of being placed on and taken off. We can only guess at the extent of this effect. However, we do know, from the history and limited data, that the set of trade restrictions was the most severe since the middle of the nineteenth century and possibly even before that time.

This study represents a synthesis of various approaches to a problem which culminated in the specification and estimation of a model relating trade and income, both driven by commercial policy and external shocks. The model gives rise to clear implications concerning the results of policy actions. The actions are summarized by the propensity of nations to restrict trade in the face of crisis. That a country's policy-makers were acting in the best interest of the nation can only be reconciled with an extremely limited view of international interaction and retaliation. That these policies were undertaken in Europe with its history of commercial policy and the evident mutuality of trade is startling. Europe failed to learn the lessons of the post–World War I period (and earlier such periods) and paid for the failure by the events following the economic collapse.

In retrospect, the policy of turning to restrictions in the face of crisis has been suicidal.

Appendix

ESTIMATED EQUATIONS AND GENERATED INCOME VALUES

All of the equations were estimated using a Hildreth-Liu autoregressive transformation, except for the large single regression packages, equations (18) and (18′), where an autoregressive method would have been inappropriate. The error associated with the last observation (1938) in one country could not have been related to the error in the next observation (1924 in the following country). All test statistics are listed in the following part, except F statistics which appear in the text.

Figures in parentheses under coefficients are T statistics. Below are the variables as they appear in the equations:

M = imports in home country currency

Y = national income in home country currency

P = relative international prices

CD or CDD = dummy variable across break date, $DD = 1930$, $D = 1931$

YDD = Y times CDD element by element (similar for YD)

EX = exchange rate cum devaluation index

TI, TII = ranking variable for tariff and nontariff restrictions; where another country name is following the variable, that country's rank variable is employed (similar for EX)

WTI = world trade index

COMM = Commonwealth trade index based upon imports

CAM = Canadian trade index based upon imports

USM = United States trade index based upon imports

$\hat{Y}$ = generated estimates of national income with actual exogenous variables

109

TABLE 19
ESTIMATED EQUATIONS, BY COUNTRY

Belgium–Luxemburg

(11) $M = -38443.56 + .500Y - 2045.92CDD + 22302.24P$
      $\qquad\qquad (5.48) \quad (-.98) \qquad\quad (3.30)$
      $\qquad dw = 2.076 \qquad\qquad R^2 = 0.953 \qquad\qquad (1924–38)$

(11'a) $M = -42474.5 + .463Y + 22688.6P$
       $\qquad\qquad (5.56) \quad (3.46)$
       $\qquad dw = 2.383 \qquad\qquad R^2 = 0.946 \qquad\qquad (1924–38)$

(11'b) $M = -1,846,080 + .428Y + 19341.6P$
       $\qquad\qquad (3.86) \quad (3.13)$
       $\qquad dw = 2.147 \qquad\qquad R^2 = 0.972 \qquad\qquad (1924–30)$

(11'c) $M = -48062.6 - 0.508 + 30212.5P$
       $\qquad\qquad (10.50) \; (3.873)$
       $\qquad dw = 2.905 \qquad\qquad R^2 = 0.978 \qquad\qquad (1931–38)$

(17) $M = -.072YDD + .518Y + 783.1P - 14.63EX - 5618.3TI$
      $\qquad\quad (-1.46) \quad (3.30) \quad (0.133) \quad (-.33) \quad\; (-2.03)$
      $\qquad\qquad\qquad\qquad\qquad\qquad\qquad\qquad\qquad\; - 6168.1TII$
      $\qquad\qquad\qquad\qquad\qquad\qquad\qquad\qquad\qquad\quad (-1.96)$
      $\qquad dw = 2.009 \qquad\qquad R^2 = 0.908 \qquad\qquad (1924–38)$

INSTRUMENTS: WTI, EXUK, TIUK, TIIUK, CDD, YUK(-1)

Bulgaria

(11) $M = -75.865 + 0.168Y - 8.750CDD + 57.834P$
      $\qquad\qquad (5.232) \quad (2.169) \qquad (2.167)$
      $\qquad dw = 1.787 \qquad\qquad R^2 = 0.897 \qquad\qquad (1924–38)$

(11'a) $M = -104.58 + 0.197Y + 68.024P$
       $\qquad\qquad (4.835) \quad (1.839)$
       $\qquad dw = 1.744 \qquad\qquad R^2 = 0.871 \qquad\qquad (1924–38)$

(11'b) $M = -250.18 + 0.379Y + 99.114P$
       $\qquad\qquad (3.338) \quad (1.422)$
       $\qquad dw = 1.742 \qquad\qquad R^2 = 0.810 \qquad\qquad (1924–30)$

(11'c) $M = -67.214 + 0.191Y + 28.160P$
       $\qquad\qquad (8.205) \quad (0.835)$
       $\qquad dw = 1.947 \qquad\qquad R^2 = 0.888 \qquad\qquad (1931–38)$

(17) $M = -044YDD + 0.208Y - 25.063P + 0.137EX - 20.350TI$
      $\qquad\quad (3.81) \qquad (7.95) \quad (1.81) \quad (2.34) \qquad (3.42)$
      $\qquad\qquad\qquad\qquad\qquad\qquad\qquad\qquad\qquad\; - 23.425TII$
      $\qquad\qquad\qquad\qquad\qquad\qquad\qquad\qquad\qquad\quad (4.66)$
      $\qquad dw = 2.223 \qquad\qquad R^2 = 0.969 \qquad\qquad (1924–38)$

INSTRUMENTS: WTI, EXGE, TIGE, TIIGE, CDD, YGE(-1)

TABLE 19—*Continued*

Czechoslovakia

(11) $M = -174.49 + 0.666Y - 27.628CDD - 96.779P$
       (6.39)   (2.15)   (1.59)
       dw = 1.941 $R^2 = 0.919$ (1924–38)

(11'a) $M = -177.88 + 0.586Y - 68.009P$
        (4.14)   (1.18)
        dw = 1.921 $R^2 = 0.904$ (1924–38)

(11'b) $M = -20.250 + 0.348Y - 36.877P$
        (0.51)   (0.18)
        dw = 1.900 $R^2 = 0.091$ (1924–30)

(11'c) $M = 36.359 + 0.312Y - 141.15P$
        (5.35)   (8.01)
        dw = 2.140 $R^2 = 0.933$ (1931–38)

(17) $M = -0.158YDD + 0.455Y - 151.70P + 0.669EX + 12.045TI$
       (2.11)   (6.68)   (3.25)   (1.01)   (1.01)
                                                    $- 5.599TII$
                                                       (0.30)
       dw = 2.267 $R^2 = 0.962$ (1924–38)

INSTRUMENTS: WTI, EXGE, TIGE, TIIGE, CDD, YGE(-1)

Denmark

(11) $M = -139347.6 + 0.572Y + 56.597CD + 417.20P$
       (6.19)   (0.66)   (1.43)
       dw = 1.596 $R^2 = 0.896$ (1924–38)

(11'a) $M = -92161.6 + 0.577Y + 416.42P$
        (6.44)   (1.47)
        dw = 1.363 $R^2 = 0.891$ (1924–38)

(11'b) $M = -92168.7 + 0.578Y + 419.34P$
        (6.53)   (1.75)
        dw = 1.458 $R^2 = 0.894$ (1924–30)

(11'c) $M = -1061.78 + 0.437Y + 1017.11P$
        (12.28)   (19.73)
        dw = 1.513 $R^2 = 0.994$ (1931–38)

(17) $M = -0.297YD + 0.514Y - 1331.3P + 1187.5TI + 1058.8TII$
       (0.85)   (2.22)   (0.73)   (0.60)   (0.66)
       dw = 1.619 $R^2 = 0.473$ (1924–38)

INSTRUMENTS: EXUK, TIUK, TIIUK, CD, YUK(-1)

TABLE 19—*Continued*

Finland

(11) $M = 8.760 + 0.395Y - 8.286CD - 22.079P$
          (8.88)   (1.55)   (1.72)
          dw = 1.841 $R^2 = 0.919$ (1924–38)

(11′a) $M = 4,144.4 + 0.623Y + 16.193P$
              (7.16)   (0.87)
              dw = 2.261 $R^2 = 0.913$ (1924–38)

(11′b) $M = 36.721 + 0.836Y - 61.992P$
              (8.57)   (3.21)
              dw = 2.250 $R^2 = 0.956$ (1924–30)

(11′c) $M = -23.760 + 0.466Y - 7.967P$
                (31.30)   (1.01)
                dw = 2.611 $R^2 = 0.989$ (1931–38)

(17) $M = 0.031YD + 0.363Y - 10.919P - 0.011EX + 4.235TI$
          (0.22)   (3.15)   (0.59)   (0.14)   (0.83)
                                                                    $- 16.274TII$
                                                                        (0.49)
          dw = 2.112 $R^2 = 0.939$ (1924–38)

INSTRUMENTS: WTI, EXUK, TIUK, TIIUK, CD, YUK(-1)

France

(11) $M = -4396.7 + 0.126Y + 5.368CD + 23.164P$
                (1.94)   (0.99)   (1.13)
                dw = 1.256 $R^2 = 0.891$ (1924–38)

(11′a) $M = -2657.3 + 0.133Y + 20.495P$
                (2.06)   (1.01)
                dw = 1.453 $R^2 = 0.881$ (1924–38)

(11′b) $M = -21.439 + 0.080Y + 50.075P$
                (9.55)   (8.51)
                dw = 2.241 $R^2 = 0.965$ (1924–30)

(11′c) $M = -27.936 + 0.018Y + 47.586P$
                (0.36)   (2.35)
                dw = 2.314 $R^2 = 0.941$ (1931–38)

(17) $M = -0.091YD + 0.175Y + 18.046P - 0.059EX - 5.200TI$
          (4.36)   (3.40)   (2.10)   (1.31)   (1.05)
                                                                    $- 1.212TII$
                                                                        (0.19)
          dw = 2.054 $R^2 = 0.946$ (1924–38)

INSTRUMENTS: WTI, EXUK, TIUK, CD, YUK(-1)

TABLE 19—*Continued*

Germany

(11) $M = 9852.2 + 0.221Y - 0.252CDD + 65.411P$
        (3.86)   (0.02)   (0.82)
        $dw = 2.724$ $R^2 = 0.884$ (1924–38)

(11′a) $M = -6793.9 + 0.252Y + 65.382P$
              (4.06)   (0.86)
          $dw = 2.720$ $R^2 = 0.884$ (1924–38)

(11′b) $M = -455.67 + 0.539Y - 159.94P$
              (4.39)   (1.76)
          $dw = 2.795$ $R^2 = 0.783$ (1924–30)

(11′c) $M = 52.262 + 0.053Y - 41.768P$
              (4.07)   (1.76)
          $dw = 2.182$ $R^2 = 0.884$ (1931–38)

(17) $M = -0.088YDD + 0.166Y + 10.333P - 6.251EX + 628.13TI$
        (4.84)   (3.27)   (0.32)   (0.41)   (0.41)
                                                                        $+ 610.97TII$
                                                                        (0.41)
        $dw = 2.051$ $R^2 = 0.870$ (1924–38)

INSTRUMENTS: WTI, EXUK, TIUK, TIIUK, CDD

Hungary

(11) $M = -1041.6 + 0.270Y - 25.241CDD - 129.85P$
            (3.16)   (0.20)   (0.35)
        $dw = 1.763$ $R^2 = 0.916$ (1924–38)

(11′a) $M = 38356.4 + 0.276Y - 116.92P$
              (3.64)   (0.35)
          $dw = 1.861$ $R^2 = 0.916$ (1924–38)

(11′b) $M = -595.44 + 0.408Y - 487.82P$
              (2.92)   (0.88)
          $dw = 2.284$ $R^2 = 0.682$ (1924–30)

(11′c) $M = -381.14 + 0.119Y + 376.14P$
              (4.42)   (1.40)
          $dw = 2.511$ $R^2 = 0.788$ (1931–38)

(17) $M = 0.009YDD + 0.326Y - 26.438P + 0.023EX - 3997.0TI$
        (0.18)   (1.69)   (0.46)   (0.13)   (0.92)
                                                                        $- 4007.5TII$
                                                                        (0.93)
        $dw = 2.023$ $R^2 = 0.915$ (1924–38)

INSTRUMENTS: WTI, CDD, YGE(−1)

TABLE 19—*Continued*

Netherlands

(11) $M = -3623.6 + 0.874Y - 187.50CD + 1404.2P$
         (31.44) (3.45) (3.66)
         $dw = 2.110$ $R^2 = 0.992$ (1924–38)

(11′a) $M = -4479.1 + 0.901Y + 2107.0P$
         (17.11) (3.97)
         $dw = 1.794$ $R^2 = 0.986$ (1924–38)

(11′b) $M = -1639.6 + 0.523Y + 1369.0P$
         (3.33) (2.06)
         $dw = 1.800$ $R^2 = 0.816$ (1924–30)

(11′c) $M = -4352.7 + 0.959Y - 1603.9P$
          (11.50) (2.36)
          $dw = 2.411$ $R^2 = 0.929$ (1931–38)

(17) $M = 0.424YD + 0.305Y + 1881.3P - 7.755EX - 2798.3TI$
        (1.70) (3.13) (1.80) (0.93) (2.36)
                                                        $- 2682.4TII$
                                                         (2.10)
         $dw = 2.790$ $R^2 = 0.993$ (1924–38)

INSTRUMENTS: WTI, CD, YUK(−1)

Sweden

(11) $M = -496.53 + 0.286Y - 105.97CD - 304.65P$
        (7.15) (1.13) (0.62)
        $dw = 2.452$ $R^2 = 0.937$ (1924–38)

(11′a) $M = 39263.5 + 0.334Y - 86.962P$
         (7.41) (0.20)
         $dw = 2.621$ $R^2 = 0.934$ (1924–38)

(11′b) $M = -1319.9 + 0.348Y + 249.28P$
         (2.51) (0.36)
         $dw = 1.116$ $R^2 = 0.852$ (1924–30)

(11′c) $M = 486.43 + 0.266Y - 1277.9P$
         (42.21) (5.94)
         $dw = 2.13$ $R^2 = 0.993$ (1931–38)

(17) $M = -0.004YD + 0.261Y - 720.25P + 2.075EX - 109.28TI$
        (0.24) (12.21) (3.09) (1.37) (1.59)
                                                        $- 134.12TII$
                                                         (1.71)
         $dw = 2.956$ $R^2 = 0.973$ (1924–38)

INSTRUMENTS: WTI, EXUK, TIUK, TIIUK, CD, YUK(−1)

TABLE 19—*Continued*

Switzerland

(11) $M = - 3273.0 + 0.284Y + 132.46CDD + 4101.3P$
           (0.80)   (0.19)   (0.768)
           $dw = 1.977$ $R^2 = 0.140$ (1924–38)

(11'a) $M = - 2668.2 + 0.265Y + 3637.9P$
           (0.85)   (0.79)
           $dw = 2.234$ $R^2 = 0.137$ (1924–38)

(11'b) $M = - 700.39 + 0.263Y + 1199.5P$
           (6.06)   (3.31)
           $dw = 2.561$ $R^2 = 0.899$ (1924–30)

(11'c) $M = - 22638.2 + 0.458Y + 29092.1P$
           (0.27)   (1.29)
           $dw = 2.638$ $R^2 = 0.285$ (1931–38)

(17) $M = - 0.127YDD + 0.562Y - 3303.5P - 9.726EX + 59.449TI$
           (0.52)   (4.38)   (1.75)   (1.44)   (0.34)
                                                                             $+ 119.07TII$
                                                                             (0.61)
           $dw = 1.112$ $R^2 = 0.939$ (1924–38)

INSTRUMENTS: CDD, TIUK, TIIUK, EXUK, WTI

United Kingdom

(11) $M = - 716.13 + 0.398Y + 85.907CDD - 683.32P$
           (5.05)   (1.56)   (2.15)
           $dw = 2.529$ $R^2 = 0.949$ (1924–38)

(11'a) $M = - 630.01 + 0.396Y - 625.92P$
           (4.73)   (1.87)
           $dw = 2.33$ $R^2 = 0.936$ (1924–38)

(11'b) $M = - 803.54 + 0.296Y + 852.75P$
           (1.23)   (2.30)
           $dw = 2.017$ $R^2 = 0.629$ (1924–30)

(11'c) $M = 890.48 + 0.211Y - 1225.9P$
           (12.22)   (5.72)
           $dw = 3.246$ $R^2 = 0.952$ (1931–38)

(17) $M = - 0.019YDD + 0.340Y - 899.83P + 2.342EX + 120.69TI$
           (1.60)   (5.13)   (2.88)   (1.40)   (1.49)
                                                                             $+ 70.378TII$
                                                                             (1.06)
           $dw = 2.478$ $R^2 = 0.969$ (1924–38)

INSTRUMENTS: CDD, WTI, COMM, CAM, USM

TABLE 20
GENERATED INCOME VALUES, BY COUNTRY

	Y	$\hat{Y}$	$\hat{Y}_1$	$\hat{Y}_2$	$\hat{Y}_3$	$\hat{Y}_1-\hat{Y}$	$\hat{Y}_2-\hat{Y}$	$\hat{Y}_3-\hat{Y}$	$\tilde{Y}_1$[a]	$\tilde{Y}_2$[b]	$\tilde{Y}_3$[c]
Belgium											
1929	74500	69139	69139	69139	69137						
1930	70990	70342	90313	70774	92438	19971	8432	22096	28.3	11.9	31.4
1931	56880	66761	89906	90764	92529	23145	24003	25768	34.6	35.0	38.5
1932	51700	51214	87823	90846	92607	36609	39632	41393	71.4	77.3	80.8
1933	51660	48691	87531	90908	92666	38840	42217	43975	79.7	86.7	90.3
1934	51510	46586	87317	89916	92745	40731	43330	46159	87.4	93.0	99.0
1935	52574	51492	87838	89152	92583	36346	37660	41091	70.5	73.1	79.8
1936	61776	60631	89070	88928	92545	28439	28297	31914	46.9	46.6	52.6
Bulgaria											
1929	562	561	561	561	561						
1930	486	474	660	693	682	186	219	208	39.2	46.2	43.8
1931	446	479	644	701	673	165	222	194	34.4	46.3	40.5
1932	393	407	630	698	662	223	225	255	54.7	55.2	62.6
1933	356	331	615	692	654	284	361	323	85.8	109.0	97.5
1934	346	333	617	697	652	284	364	319	85.2	109.3	95.7
1935	366	375	620	694	656	245	319	281	65.3	85.0	74.9
1936	402	387	621	688	664	234	301	277	60.4	77.7	71.5

	Y	$\hat{Y}$	$\hat{Y}_1$	$\hat{Y}_2$	$\hat{Y}_3$	$\hat{Y}_1 - \hat{Y}$	$\hat{Y}_2 - \hat{Y}$	$\hat{Y}_3 - \hat{Y}$	$\tilde{Y}_1$	$\tilde{Y}_2$	$\tilde{Y}_3$
					Czechoslovakia						
1929	676.2	675.9	675.9	675.9	675.9						
1930	684.7	703.6	943.5	793.0	940.5	239.9	89.4	236.9	34.0	12.7	33.6
1931	637.2	641.1	929.3	834.2	942.9	288.2	193.1	301.8	44.9	30.1	47.0
1932	567.3	531.0	914.2	843.5	952.2	383.2	312.5	421.2	72.1	58.8	79.3
1933	568.0	573.9	991.4	920.5	1029.2	417.5	346.6	455.3	72.7	60.3	79.3
1934	533.6	525.0	910.1	873.1	959.9	385.1	348.1	434.9	73.3	66.3	82.8
1935	526.3	528.5	902.7	871.1	954.9	374.2	342.6	426.4	70.8	64.8	80.6
1936	528.3	551.9	894.8	867.6	946.5	342.9	315.7	394.6	62.1	57.2	71.4
					Denmark						
1930	4249	4604	4604	4604	4604						
1931	4660	4821	5117	5210	5084	296	389	263	6.0	8.0	5.4
1932	4353	4239	5143	5414	5289	904	1175	1050	21.3	27.7	24.7
1933	4712	4617	5538	5350	5476	921	733	859	19.9	15.8	18.6
1934	5092	5188	5945	5537	5662	757	349	474	14.5	6.7	9.1
1935	5422	5296	6100	5501	5626	804	205	330	15.1	3.8	6.2
1936	5861	5709	6209	5459	5584	500	—d	—	8.7	—	—

a. $\tilde{Y}_1 = \dfrac{\hat{Y}_1 - \hat{Y}}{\hat{Y}}$ %; policy effect on income

b. $\tilde{Y}_2 = \dfrac{\hat{Y}_2 - \hat{Y}}{\hat{Y}}$ %; taste effect on income

c. $\tilde{Y}_3 = \dfrac{\hat{Y}_3 - \hat{Y}}{\hat{Y}}$ %; total trade effect on income

d. — (Negative % $\triangle$)

TABLE 20—Continued

	Y	$\hat{Y}$	$\hat{Y}_1$	$\hat{Y}_2$	$\hat{Y}_3$	$\hat{Y}_1-\hat{Y}$	$\hat{Y}_2-\hat{Y}$	$\hat{Y}_3-\hat{Y}$	$\tilde{Y}_1$	$\tilde{Y}_2$	$\tilde{Y}_3$
Finland											
1930	200	176	176	176	176	—	—	—	—	—	—
1931	174	168	191	219	191	23	51	23	13.6	30.3	13.6
1932	173	175	199	226	199	24	51	24	13.7	29.1	13.7
1933	183	189	199	227	200	10	38	11	5.2	20.1	5.8
1934	212	211	198	228	201	—	17	—	—	8.0	—
1935	224	225	195	226	199	—	1	—	—	0.4	—
1936	250	247	190	223	197	—	—	—	—	—	—
France											
1930	243	244	244	244	244	—	—	—	—	—	—
1931	229	274	347	343	355	73	69	81	26.6	25.1	29.5
1932	206	200	341	349	361	141	149	161	70.5	74.5	80.5
1933	199	192	341	353	364	149	161	172	77.6	83.3	89.5
1934	184	155	338	358	369	183	203	214	118.0	130.9	138.0
1935	176	175	349	395	384	174	220	209	99.4	125.7	119.4
1936	195	198	346	381	372	148	183	174	74.7	92.4	87.8
Germany											
1929	759	712	712	712	712	—	—	—	—	—	—
1930	702	743	907	891	911	164	148	168	22.0	19.9	22.6
1931	575	544	959	971	1025	415	427	481	76.4	78.4	88.4
1932	452	373	903	970	1027	530	597	654	142.0	160.0	175.3
1933	462	462	907	1079	1026	445	617	564	96.3	133.5	122.0
1934	572	490	956	1042	1022	466	552	532	95.1	112.6	108.5
1935	586	447	962	1006	1022	515	556	575	115.2	125.0	128.6
1936	658	571	1000	1003	1025	429	432	454	75.1	75.6	79.5

Hungary

	Y	$\hat{Y}$	$\hat{Y}_1$	$\hat{Y}_2$	$\hat{Y}_3$	$\hat{Y}_1-\hat{Y}$	$\hat{Y}_2-\hat{Y}$	$\hat{Y}_3-\hat{Y}$	$\tilde{Y}_1$	$\tilde{Y}_2$	$\tilde{Y}_3$
1929	5039	4550	4550	4550	4550						
1930	4317	3690	4429	4420	4423	739	730	733	20.0	19.7	19.8
1931	3681	2849	4454	4431	4431	1605	1582	1582	56.3	55.5	55.5
1932	3467	2212	4465	4437	4441	2253	2225	2229	101.8	100.5	100.7
1933	3374	2155	4457	4426	4431	2302	2271	2276	106.8	105.3	105.6
1934	3491	2252	4458	4430	4435	2206	2178	2183	97.9	96.7	96.9
1935	3805	2423	4454	4438	4445	2031	2015	2022	83.8	83.1	83.4
1936	4202	2514	4439	4433	4441	1925	1919	1927	76.5	76.3	76.6

Netherlands

	Y	$\hat{Y}$	$\hat{Y}_1$	$\hat{Y}_2$	$\hat{Y}_3$	$\hat{Y}_1-\hat{Y}$	$\hat{Y}_2-\hat{Y}$	$\hat{Y}_3-\hat{Y}$	$\tilde{Y}_1$	$\tilde{Y}_2$	$\tilde{Y}_3$
1930	5860	5657	5657	5657	5657						
1931	5129	5160	7171	6242	6432	2011	1082	1272	38.9	20.9	24.6
1932	4558	4372	8279	6555	6740	3907	2183	2368	89.3	49.9	54.1
1933	4391	4661	8470	6887	6697	3809	2226	2036	81.7	47.7	43.6
1934	4340	4051	8418	6761	6574	4367	2710	2523	107.8	66.8	62.2
1935	4251	4122	8845	7063	6876	4723	2941	2754	114.5	71.3	66.8
1936	4359	4290	8866	7106	7049	4576	2816	2759	106.6	65.6	64.3

Sweden

	Y	$\hat{Y}$	$\hat{Y}_1$	$\hat{Y}_2$	$\hat{Y}_3$	$\hat{Y}_1-\hat{Y}$	$\hat{Y}_2-\hat{Y}$	$\hat{Y}_3-\hat{Y}$	$\tilde{Y}_1$	$\tilde{Y}_2$	$\tilde{Y}_3$
1930	8137	8072	8072	8072	8072						
1931	7387	7473	8308	8318	8318	835	845	845	11.1	11.3	11.3
1932	6481	6934	8510	8832	8534	1576	1898	1600	22.7	27.3	23.0
1933	6840	6806	8571	8922	8589	1765	2116	1783	25.9	31.0	26.1
1934	7784	7875	8792	9183	8796	917	1308	921	11.6	16.6	11.6
1935	8295	8392	8738	9041	8735	346	649	343	4.1	7.7	4.0
1936	9107	8898	8652	8937	8636	—	39	—	—	0.4	—

TABLE 20—Continued

	Y	$\hat{\hat{Y}}$	$\hat{Y}_1$	$\hat{Y}_2$	$\hat{Y}_3$	$\hat{Y}_1-\hat{\hat{Y}}$	$\hat{Y}_2-\hat{\hat{Y}}$	$\hat{Y}_3-\hat{\hat{Y}}$	$\tilde{Y}_1$	$\tilde{Y}_2$	$\tilde{Y}_3$
					Switzerland						
1929	9469	9068	9068	9068	9068						
1930	9344	8984	9032	9263	9095	48	279	111	0.5	3.1	1.2
1931	8609	8133	9131	8986	9025	998	853	926	12.2	10.4	11.3
1932	7685	7348	9225	8868	8907	1877	1520	1559	25.5	20.6	21.2
1933	7698	6995	9181	8820	8866	2186	1825	1871	31.2	26.0	26.7
1934	7599	6715	9192	8807	8854	2477	2092	2139	36.8	31.1	31.8
1935	7429	6427	9073	8752	8696	2646	2325	2269	40.8	36.1	35.3
1936	7457	6233	9037	8594	8666	2804	2361	2433	44.9	37.8	39.0
					United Kingdom						
1929	4178	4233	4233	4233	4233						
1930	3957	3998	4528	4027	4548	530	29	550	13.2	0.7	13.7
1931	3666	3701	4501	4190	4535	800	489	834	21.6	13.2	22.5
1932	3568	3596	4683	4492	4723	1087	896	1127	30.2	24.9	31.3
1933	3728	3653	4785	4597	4815	1132	944	1162	30.9	25.8	31.8
1934	3881	3963	4983	4726	4914	930	763	951	23.4	19.2	23.9
1935	4109	4186	4836	4860	4843	650	674	657	15.5	16.1	15.6
1936	4388	4412	4813	4820	4804	401	408	392	9.0	9.2	8.8

DATA

Currency units refer to income (Y), exports (X), and imports (M) only. Price (P) and exchange rate (EX) data are indices. For income data, extrapolation and interpolation of some dates were used for a few series. World trade index (WTI), Canadian trade (CAM), Commonwealth trade (COMM), and United States trade (USM) are all converted into equivalent pound valuations at the appropriate exchange rate for each year. The tariff level rates are all ad valorem.

TABLE 21
INCOME, TRADE, PRICE, AND EXCHANGE RATE DATA, BY COUNTRY

	Y	X	M	P	EX
		Belgium–Luxemburg			
		(million francs)			
1924	32250	13812	17700	1.000	24.1
1925	35250	14748	17856	.963	24.7
1926	43300	19932	23040	1.184	17.5
1927	50760	26628	29076	1.350	100.1
1928	62430	30876	31980	1.351	100.2
1929	74500	31764	35424	1.384	100.1
1930	70990	26244	30924	1.371	100.3
1931	58660	23064	23748	1.311	100.2
1932	51700	14808	16164	1.259	100.1
1933	51660	14004	14820	1.220	100.2
1934	51510	13536	13704	1.168	99.9
1935	52594	15792	17112	1.275	78.6
1936	61776	19524	21300	1.300	72.0
1937	67526	25392	27252	1.314	71.7
1938	67500	21636	22620	1.225	71.8
		Bulgaria			
		(hundred million leva)			
1924	437	58.8	56.4	1.000	3.8
1925	495	62.4	78.0	.990	4.2
1926	494	52.8	56.4	.922	3.7
1927	525	66.0	61.2	.947	3.7
1928	555	62.4	70.8	1.021	3.7
1929	562	63.6	82.8	1.098	99.9
1930	486	62.4	45.6	1.007	99.8
1931	446	58.8	46.8	.943	99.2
1932	393	33.6	34.8	.918	99.6
1933	356	28.8	21.6	.863	97.1
1934	346	25.2	21.6	.887	96.2
1935	366	32.4	30.0	.876	98.4
1936	402	39.6	32.4	.826	98.8
1937	466	50.4	49.2	.819	99.7
1938	513	55.2	46.8	.857	99.1

TABLE 21—*Continued*

	Y	X	M	P	EX
			Czechoslovakia (hundred million Kc)		
1924	633.4	169.2	158.4	1.000	14.6
1925	657.3	188.4	176.4	.993	14.6
1926	648.1	177.6	152.4	.872	14.6
1927	653.2	201.6	180.0	.896	14.6
1928	665.5	212.4	192.0	.899	14.6
1929	676.2	205.2	199.2	.858	14.6
1930	684.7	175.2	157.2	.884	100.0
1931	637.0	130.8	117.6	.891	100.0
1932	567.3	73.2	74.4	.919	100.0
1933	568.0	58.8	58.8	1.150	100.0
1934	533.6	73.2	63.6	.942	85.4
1935	526.8	74.4	67.2	.927	83.4
1936	528.3	80.4	79.2	.902	80.1
1937	600.8	120.0	109.2	.833	69.6
1938	566.6	112.8	92.4	.823	69.1
			Denmark (million kroner)		
1924	4986	1980	2220	1.000	62.4
1925	4937	1788	1932	.829	78.9
1926	4540	1404	1524	.594	97.8
1927	4736	1452	1584	.559	99.7
1928	4841	1548	1644	.562	99.8
1929	5035	1620	1716	.559	99.6
1930	4929	1524	1632	.549	99.9
1931	4660	1260	1416	.547	93.5
1932	4353	1092	1104	.626	70.3
1933	4712	1164	1224	.698	55.8
1934	5092	1176	1308	.770	50.1
1935	5422	1212	1284	.756	48.5
1936	5681	1332	1440	.740	49.0
1937	6094	1536	1644	.727	48.6
1938	6360	1584	1656	.695	48.1

TABLE 21—*Continued*

	Y	X	M	P	EX

Finland
(hundred million markka)

	Y	X	M	P	EX
1924	173	50.4	46.8	1.000	14.1
1925	188	55.2	55.2	1.074	13.1
1926	192	56.4	56.4	1.177	100.1
1927	214	63.6	63.6	1.204	100.0
1928	226	62.4	80.4	1.210	100.0
1929	216	64.8	69.6	1.177	99.9
1930	200	54.0	52.8	1.229	99.9
1931	174	44.4	34.8	1.299	94.8
1932	173	46.8	34.8	1.558	61.7
1933	183	52.8	39.6	1.598	58.1
1934	212	62.4	48.0	1.647	52.8
1935	224	62.4	54.0	1.583	51.0
1936	250	72.0	63.6	1.497	51.5
1937	303	93.6	93.6	1.451	51.2
1938	313	90.0	85.2	1.408	50.6

France
(hundred million francs)

	Y	X	M	P	EX
1924	128	42.0	39.6	1.000	27.1
1925	134	46.8	44.4	1.111	24.7
1926	208	58.8	60.0	1.307	16.8
1927	210	55.2	55.2	1.161	20.3
1928	227	51.6	54.0	1.169	99.8
1929	245	50.4	58.8	1.171	100.0
1930	243	43.2	52.8	1.165	100.2
1931	229	30.0	42.0	1.208	100.1
1932	206	19.2	30.0	1.149	100.3
1933	199	18.0	28.8	1.117	100.0
1934	184	26.4	22.8	1.069	100.0
1935	176	36.0	20.4	.924	100.0
1936	195	28.8	25.2	1.042	92.4
1937	275	30.0	42.0	1.282	61.0
1938	369	34.8	45.6	1.458	43.4

TABLE 21—*Continued*

	Y	X	M	P	EX
			Germany		
		(hundred million Reich marks)			
1924	510	66.0	91.2	1.000	00.1
1925	600	87.6	123.6	1.021	99.9
1926	627	98.4	99.6	.890	99.9
1927	708	102.0	142.8	.918	99.8
1928	754	116.4	140.4	.936	100.2
1929	759	127.2	134.4	.930	99.4
1930	702	112.8	104.4	.961	100.1
1931	575	92.4	67.2	.970	99.2
1932	452	56.4	46.8	.936	99.7
1933	462	49.2	42.0	.945	99.6
1934	572	42.0	44.4	1.010	98.6
1935	586	43.2	42.0	1.010	100.3
1936	658	48.0	42.0	.959	100.1
1937	738	58.8	55.2	.850	99.7
1938	821	58.8	60.0	.860	99.6
			Hungary		
		(million pengo)			
1924	4337	667.2	814.8	1.000	00.1
1925	4870	847.2	864.0	1.016	00.1
1926	5178	877.2	940.8	.825	00.4
1927	5133	807.6	1182.0	.873	99.9
1928	5414	825.6	1212.0	.905	99.7
1929	5039	1038.0	1063.2	.830	99.1
1930	4317	912.0	823.2	.748	100.0
1931	3681	570.0	540.0	.841	99.8
1932	3467	334.8	328.8	.909	99.8
1933	3374	391.2	313.2	.774	99.1
1934	3491	404.4	344.4	.826	98.8
1935	3805	451.2	402.0	.894	99.2
1936	4202	504.0	436.8	.832	99.8
1937	4368	588.0	475.2	.763	99.4
1938	4617	522.0	405.6	.781	99.3

TABLE 21—*Continued*

	Y	X	M	P	EX
			Netherlands		
			(million gulden)		
1924	5234	1656	2364	1.000	95.1
1925	5394	1812	2460	.981	99.9
1926	5508	1776	2436	.847	99.8
1927	5603	1896	2544	.866	99.8
1928	5979	1992	2688	.877	100.1
1929	6108	1980	2748	.848	99.9
1930	5860	1716	2424	.792	100.1
1931	5129	1308	1872	.839	100.1
1932	4558	852	1296	.789	100.3
1933	4391	720	1212	.796	100.1
1934	4340	708	1044	.816	100.0
1935	4251	672	936	.767	100.0
1936	4359	744	1020	.739	94.9
1937	4802	1152	1548	.762	80.9
1938	4904	1044	1416	.729	80.8
			Sweden		
			(million kroner)		
1924	7170	1261.2	1424.4	1.000	99.0
1925	7311	1359.6	1446.0	.981	100.2
1926	7499	1419.6	1490.4	.839	99.9
1927	7663	1856.4	1584.0	.823	100.1
1928	7871	1574.4	1707.6	.839	100.0
1929	8220	1812.0	1771.2	.805	99.9
1930	8137	1550.4	1647.6	.795	100.2
1931	7387	1122.0	1428.0	.823	94.2
1932	6481	948.0	1154.4	.901	68.9
1933	6840	1078.8	1095.6	.921	64.5
1934	7784	1302.0	1304.4	.996	57.8
1935	8295	1297.2	1476.0	.974	56.0
1936	9107	1514.4	1633.2	.938	56.6
1937	10274	2000.4	2122.8	.931	56.2
1938	10704	1812.0	2088.0	.894	55.5

TABLE 21—*Continued*

	Y	X	M	P	EX
			Switzerland (million francs)		
1924	7738	2070.0	2504.4	1.000	94.4
1925	8443	2038.8	2632,8	.924	100.2
1926	8528	1836.0	2414.4	.772	100.1
1927	9154	2023.2	2564.4	.758	99.8
1928	9673	2134.8	2744.4	.778	99.8
1929	9469	2104.8	2784.0	.767	99.8
1930	9344	1767.6	2664.0	.783	100.4
1931	8609	1348.8	2251.2	.771	100.6
1932	7685	801.6	1762.8	.751	100.6
1933	7698	853.2	1594.8	.744	100.2
1934	7599	843.6	1434.0	.742	100.1
1935	7429	822.0	1282.8	.715	100.0
1936	7457	882.0	1266.0	.710	92.6
1937	8160	1285.2	1807.2	.714	70.2
1938	8202	1316.4	1606.8	.696	70.0
			United Kingdom (million pounds)		
1924	3919	800.4	1137.6	1.000	90.7
1925	3980	772.8	1166.4	.944	99.2
1926	3914	652.8	1116.0	.812	99.2
1927	4145	709.2	1095.6	.780	99.9
1928	4154	723.6	1075.2	.773	100.0
1929	4178	729.6	1111.2	.768	99.8
1930	3957	571.2	955.2	.763	99.9
1931	3666	391.2	798.0	.758	93.1
1932	3568	364.8	650.4	.830	71.8
1933	3728	368.4	626.4	.865	68.1
1934	3881	396.0	680.4	.903	61.8
1935	4109	426.0	700.8	.876	59.8
1936	4388	440.4	787.2	.861	60.5
1937	4616	522.0	952.8	.815	60.0
1938	4640	470.4	859.2	.818	59.3

SOURCES: Y: 42, 34; X, M: 41; P: 41, 44; EX: 41, 38; WTI: 47; CAM, COMM, USM: 39, 41; tariffs: 28, 45, 34, 18.

TABLE 22
World, U.S., Commonwealth, and Canadian Trade Data

	WTI[a]	USM[b]	COMM[b]	CAM[b]
1924	76.9	843	255	188
1925	81.0	901	265	192
1926	82.6	945	280	216
1927	89.9	892	273	233
1928	97.2	873	256	261
1929	100.0	930	255	276
1930	92.6	667	197	216
1931	84.5	480	116	139
1932	74.2	395	106	119
1933	75.4	450	125	92
1934	78.0	566	161	107
1935	81.8	729	185	116
1936	85.6	857	214	133
1937	96.5	1,073	257	170
1938	89.0	703	254	142

a. 1929 = 100
b. £ 000,000

TABLE 23
European Tariff Levels, by Country

	1925	1927	1931
Belgium		11.1	18.4
Bulgaria		56.5	96.0
Czechoslovakia		31.3	49.6
Denmark	6.0		
Finland		31.6	48.2
France		23.1	37.9
Germany		20.4	40.7
Great Britain	4.0		
Hungary		34.9	45.1
Netherlands	4.0		
Sweden		20.1	27.8
Switzerland		16.9	21.7

TABLE 24
TRADE BALANCES BY COUNTRY, 1928, 1935, 1938
(Postdevaluation dollars, 000,000)

	1928			1935			1938		
	X	M	B	X	M	B	X	M	B
Belgium–Luxemburg									
Austria	6	2	4	2	2	0	2	2	0
Belgium–Lux.*	—	—	—	—	—	—	—	—	—
Czechoslovakia*	6	6	0	3	6	− 3	6	8	− 2
France*	190	318	−128	105	98	7	110	112	− 2
Germany*	199	188	11	58	78	−20	90	89	1
Italy	32	18	14	16	7	9	9	7	2
Netherlands*	194	175	19	65	59	6	88	71	17
Sweden*	12	15	− 3	12	9	3	20	16	4
Switzerland*	36	14	22	16	7	9	19	9	10
Bulgaria*	3	1	2	1	0	1	1	0	1
Denmark*	15	1	14	5	4	1	6	4	+ 2
Estonia	4	12	− 8	2	5	− 3	3	4	− 1
Finland*	8	25	− 17	4	10	− 6	7	8	− 1
Greece	9	2	7	1	1	0	2	1	1
Hungary*	1	1	0	0	1	− 1	1	1	0
Norway	10	13	− 3	7	6	1	9	6	3
Poland	7	12	− 5	6	11	− 5	10	10	0
Portugal	8	5	3	6	2	4	6	3	3
Roumania	4	6	− 2	1	1	0	4	4	0
Spain	14	10	4	9	6	3	8	3	5
Turkey	9	2	7	0	2	− 2	2	2	0
Yugoslavia	1	1	0	0	3	− 3	1	5	− 4
United Kingdom*	257	170	87	82	50	32	98	61	37
Rest of World	418	498	− 80	159	235	−76	201	312	−111
Europe	1031	998	33	406	369	37	508	426	82
Group	921	914	7	351	322	29	446	379	67
Total	1451	1506	− 55	572	625	−53	724	765	−41

*Group member nations

TABLE 24—*Continued*

	1928			1935			1938		
	X	M	B	X	M	B	X	M	B
				Czechoslovakia					
Austria	156	71	85	32	13	19	9	8	1
Belgium–Lux.*	8	15	− 7	7	7	0	7	7	0
Czechoslovakia*	—	—	—	—	—	—	—	—	—
France*	14	41	−27	13	16	− 3	9	13	− 4
Germany*	284	371	−87	50	63	−13	59	55	4
Italy	40	32	8	10	10	0	13	8	5
Netherlands*	19	14	5	12	12	0	15	9	6
Sweden*	15	13	2	8	6	2	10	12	− 2
Switzerland*	31	24	7	11	8	3	12	10	2
Bulgaria*	9	4	5	4	3	1	2	3	− 1
Denmark*	14	2	12	3	2	1	2	1	1
Estonia	7	3	4	2	2	0	3	2	1
Finland*	5	0	5	2	0	2	4	1	3
Greece	7	3	4	3	3	0	1	4	− 3
Hungary*	74	43	31	6	6	0	9	6	3
Norway	5	2	3	3	2	1	5	2	3
Poland	44	63	−19	11	11	0	7	9	− 2
Portugal	1	1	0	1	1	0	—	1	− 1
Roumania	44	27	−17	16	11	5	19	17	2
Spain	5	5	0	3	3	0	—	—	0
Turkey	9	3	6	3	3	0	10	5	5
Yugoslavia	47	23	24	13	15	− 2	23	11	12
United Kingdom*	74	42	32	23	16	7	32	16	16
Rest of World	135	148	−13	69	65	4	84	89	− 5
Europe	912	802	110	236	213	23	261	200	61
Group	547	569	−22	139	139	0	161	133	28
Total	1061	960	101	309	281	28	354	292	62

TABLE 24—*Continued*

	1928			1935			1938		
	X	M	B	X	M	B	X	M	B
				France					
Austria	13	17	− 4	5	6	− 1	4	4	0
Belgium–Lux.*	529	268	261	121	93	28	120	90	30
Czechoslovakia*	13	14	− 1	13	13	0	12	9	3
France*	—	—	—	—	—	—	—	—	—
Germany*	373	332	41	70	116	−46	53	90	−37
Italy	141	101	40	40	27	13	14	17	− 3
Netherlands*	89	113	−24	31	35	− 4	38	34	4
Sweden*	19	43	−24	12	19	− 7	14	19	− 5
Switzerland*	214	62	152	69	34	35	55	29	26
Bulgaria*	4	2	2	0	1	− 1	2	1	1
Denmark*	20	6	14	9	3	6	5	3	2
Estonia	6	9	− 3	0	3	− 3	3	3	0
Finland*	7	23	−16	3	9	− 6	4	8	− 4
Greece	30	8	22	2	2	0	2	2	0
Hungary*	3	2	1	1	2	− 1	1	3	− 2
Norway	8	15	− 7	6	8	− 2	7	9	− 2
Poland	29	14	15	8	10	− 2	10	3	7
Portugal	15	17	− 2	6	7	− 1	6	8	− 2
Roumania	10	13	− 3	7	10	− 3	10	6	4
Spain	112	108	4	20	23	− 3	11	6	5
Turkey	32	12	20	3	2	1	2	4	− 2
Yugoslavia	5	8	− 3	4	2	2	4	3	1
United Kingdom*	524	352	172	107	105	2	102	92	10
Rest of World	1243	1963	−720	474	838	−364	388	864	−476
Europe	2202	1540	662	540	530	10	483	453	30
Group	1795	1217	578	436	430	6	406	378	28
Total	3456	3551	−95	1026	1393	−367	876	1322	−446

TABLE 24—*Continued*

	1928			1935			1938		
	X	M	B	X	M	B	X	M	B
				Germany					
Austria	172	94	78	44	29	15	47	35	12
Belgium–Lux.*	197	191	6	81	51	30	92	78	14
Czechoslovakia*	261	217	44	52	49	3	55	52	3
France*	325	387	−62	105	72	33	88	58	30
Germany*	—	—	—	—	—	—	—	—	—
Italy	221	188	33	111	76	35	121	99	22
Netherlands*	874	287	587	163	79	84	180	80	100
Sweden*	174	102	72	83	62	21	107	106	1
Switzerland*	231	133	98	104	46	58	83	42	41
Bulgaria*	15	21	− 6	16	17	− 1	23	34	−11
Denmark*	168	142	26	57	48	9	81	67	14
Estonia	69	62	7	19	19	0	35	38	− 3
Finland*	86	51	35	20	17	3	33	36	− 3
Greece	24	38	−14	20	24	− 4	45	38	7
Hungary*	62	29	33	25	31	− 6	44	44	0
Norway	68	49	19	35	38	− 3	50	40	10
Poland	200	152	48	25	30	− 5	54	44	10
Portugal	20	15	5	12	9	3	16	10	6
Roumania	70	76	− 6	26	32	− 6	60	56	4
Spain	84	112	−28	42	45	− 3	31	37	− 6
Turkey	27	29	− 2	27	38	−11	61	47	14
Yugoslavia	48	27	21	15	25	−10	48	44	4
United Kingdom*	476	360	116	151	103	48	140	113	27
Rest of World	1198	2897	−1699	463	641	−178	640	999	−359
Europe	3487	2766	721	1240	945	349	1509	1204	305
Group	2869	1920	949	858	575	282	926	710	216
Total	4848	5663	−815	1719	1667	52	2162	2222	−60

TABLE 24—*Continued*

	1928			1935			1938		
	X	M	B	X	M	B	X	M	B

Netherlands

Austria	9	5	4	3	3	0	3	4	1
Belgium–Lux.*	119	205	−86	49	70	−21	58	88	−30
Czechoslovakia*	10	16	− 6	7	12	− 5	7	16	− 9
France*	82	82	0	32	30	2	33	36	− 3
Germany*	314	498	−184	87	164	−77	84	165	−81
Italy	24	12	12	11	8	3	7	7	0
Netherlands*	—	—	—	—	—	—	—	—	—
Sweden*	20	28	− 8	14	10	4	20	17	3
Switzerland*	17	16	1	12	7	5	12	12	0
Bulgaria*	1	1	0	0	1	− 1	0	0	0
Denmark*	21	5	16	3	3	0	4	6	− 2
Estonia	2	10	− 8	2	3	− 1	4	4	0
Finland*	11	22	−11	3	4	− 1	5	9	− 4
Greece	4	5	− 1	2	2	0	2	2	0
Hungary*	3	1	2	1	1	0	1	2	− 1
Norway	19	6	13	5	4	1	9	7	2
Poland	16	18	− 2	5	8	− 3	7	12	− 5
Portugal	5	5	0	3	1	2	3	2	1
Roumania	3	5	− 2	1	1	0	1	2	− 1
Spain	14	13	1	10	6	4	4	2	2
Turkey	6	3	3	1	1	0	1	2	− 1
Yugoslavia	1	1	0	1	1	0	1	2	− 1
United Kingdom*	292	175	117	97	60	37	129	63	66
Rest of World	331	677	−346	99	218	−119	157	188	−31
Europe	997	1133	−136	352	401	−49	398	461	−63
Group	890	1049	−159	305	362	−57	353	414	−61
Total	1331	1826	−495	458	635	−117	568	774	−206

TABLE 24—*Continued*

	1928			1935			1938		
	X	M	B	X	M	B	X	M	B
			Sweden						
Austria	3	3	0	1	2	1	4	3	− 2
Belgium–Lux.*	17	18	− 1	10	12	− 2	14	22	− 8
Czechoslovakia*	7	11	− 4	3	7	− 4	9	11	− 2
France*	41	27	14	14	12	2	5	16	−11
Germany*	90	241	−151	48	91	−43	82	121	−39
Italy	10	9	1	8	6	2	10	8	2
Netherlands*	32	31	1	10	19	− 9	17	29	−12
Sweden*	—	—	—	—	—	—	—	—	—
Switzerland*	3	8	− 5	2	6	− 4	3	11	− 8
Bulgaria*	0	0	0	0	0	0	0	0	0
Denmark*	46	52	− 6	19	25	− 6	22	29	− 7
Estonia	7	6	1	2	2	0	5	3	2
Finland*	27	5	22	11	5	6	22	5	17
Greece	3	1	2	2	4	− 2	2	1	1
Hungary*	1	1	0	0	1	− 1	—	4	− 3
Norway	39	20	19	17	13	4	31	16	15
Poland	13	14	− 1	4	12	− 8	9	18	− 9
Portugal	1	3	− 2	1	1	0	1	1	0
Roumania	2	0	2	1	0	1	1	1	0
Spain	18	5	13	7	4	3	1	0	1
Turkey	3	1	2	2	1	1	2	1	1
Yugoslavia	0	0	0	0	0	0	1	0	1
United Kingdom*	179	125	54	82	73	9	113	96	17
Rest of World	155	183	−33	81	74	7	93	121	−28
Europe	546	583	−37	246	297	−51	366	399	−33
Group	442	519	−75	199	251	−52	288	344	−56
Total	715	775	−60	330	375	−45	463	523	−60

TABLE 24—*Continued*

	1928			1935			1938		
	X	M	B	X	M	B	X	M	B
				Switzerland					
Austria	22	19	3	7	9	− 2	7	8	− 1
Belgium–Lux.*	14	31	−17	7	12	− 5	10	16	− 6
Czechoslovakia*	17	31	−14	7	13	− 6	10	13	− 3
France*	51	159	−108	32	60	−28	28	51	−23
Germany*	123	203	−80	55	110	−55	47	84	−37
Italy	43	65	−22	24	30	− 6	21	27	− 6
Netherlands*	18	17	1	8	12	− 4	14	13	1
Sweden*	9	4	5	5	4	1	9	4	5
Switzerland*	—	—	—	—	—	—	—	—	—
Bulgaria*	1	2	− 1	2	1	1	1	1	0
Denmark*	6	8	− 2	3	4	− 1	4	3	1
Estonia	2	0	2	1	2	− 1	3	1	2
Finland*	2	0	2	1	1	0	3	0	3
Greece	3	2	1	1	1	0	1	1	0
Hungary*	6	6	0	4	5	− 1	3	6	− 3
Norway	4	1	3	1	1	0	3	2	1
Poland	16	8	8	5	6	− 1	5	6	− 1
Portugal	3	1	2	2	1	1	2	1	1
Roumania	6	5	1	4	12	− 8	3	6	− 3
Spain	27	16	11	7	8	− 1	1	1	0
Turkey	3	2	1	1	2	− 1	1	1	0
Yugoslavia	4	5	− 1	2	3	− 1	3	3	0
United Kingdom*	100	46	54	25	25	0	34	20	14
Rest of World	207	233	−26	54	84	−30	85	88	− 3
Europe	481	632	−151	204	323	−119	213	268	−55
Group	347	507	−160	149	247	−98	163	211	−48
Total	690	867	−177	259	410	−151	301	363	−62

TABLE 24—*Continued*

	1928			1935			1938		
	X	M	B	X	M	B	X	M	B
			Bulgaria						
Austria	11	7	— 4	2	2	0	5	3	2
Belgium–Lux.*	3	3	0	0	0	0	1	0	1
Czechoslovakia*	2	9	— 7	3	4	— 1	3	4	— 1
France*	5	7	— 2	1	1	0	1	2	— 1
Germany*	21	18	3	19	20	— 1	35	28	7
Italy	9	13	— 4	3	1	2	5	5	0
Netherlands*	3	2	1	1	1	0	1	1	0
Sweden*	0	1	— 1	1	0	1	0	1	— 1
Switzerland*	1	2	— 1	1	2	— 1	1	1	0
Bulgaria*	—	—	—	—	—	—	—	—	—
Denmark*	0	0	0	1	0	1	2	0	2
Estonia	0	0	0	0	0	0	0	0	0
Finland*	0	0	0	0	0	0	0	0	0
Greece	6	1	5	0	0	0	1	0	1
Hungary*	2	2	0	1	1	0	1	2	— 1
Norway	0	0	0	0	0	0	0	0	0
Poland	3	1	2	1	0	1	4	3	1
Portugal	0	0	0	0	0	0	0	0	0
Roumania	2	5	— 3	0	1	— 1	0	2	— 2
Spain	0	0	0	1	1	0	0	0	0
Turkey	4	2	2	0	0	0	1	1	0
Yugoslavia	0	1	— 1	0	0	0	0	0	0
United Kingdom*	2	9	— 7	2	2	0	3	4	— 1
Rest of World	2	3	— 1	3	1	2	4	3	1
Europe	74	83	— 9	37	36	1	64	57	7
Group	39	53	—14	30	31	— 1	47	42	5
Total	76	86	—10	40	37	3	68	60	8

TABLE 24—*Continued*

	1928			1935			1938		
	X	M	B	X	M	B	X	M	B
				Denmark					
Austria	1	2	− 1	1	1	0	1	1	0
Belgium–Lux.*	2	20	−18	4	6	− 2	5	8	− 3
Czechoslovakia*	1	8	− 7	2	2	0	1	2	− 1
France*	5	29	−24	3	8	− 5	5	4	1
Germany*	155	257	−102	45	65	−20	66	87	−21
Italy	4	5	− 1	2	2	0	1	3	− 2
Netherlands*	6	32	−26	3	9	− 6	6	14	− 8
Sweden*	49	50	− 1	18	20	− 2	17	23	− 6
Switzerland*	8	6	2	3	3	0	3	4	− 1
Bulgaria*	0	0	0	0	1	− 1	0	1	− 1
Denmark*	—	—	—	—	—	—	—	—	—
Estonia	5	3	2	1	2	− 1	2	1	1
Finland*	13	7	6	4	5	− 1	5	7	− 2
Greece	1	0	1	0	0	0	0	1	− 1
Hungary*	0	0	0	0	0	0	0	1	− 1
Norway	31	13	18	12	7	5	9	9	0
Poland	9	12	− 3	2	6	− 4	2	4	− 2
Portugal	1	2	− 1	1	1	0	0	1	− 1
Roumania	0	6	− 6	0	1	− 1	3	2	1
Spain	2	3	− 1	2	3	− 1	0	0	0
Turkey	0	0	0	0	0	0	0	1	− 1
Yugoslavia	0	0	0	0	0	0	0	0	0
United Kingdom*	416	109	307	161	105	56	188	123	65
Rest of World	30	208	−178	11	38	−27	19	51	−32
Europe	718	566	152	268	248	20	316	298	18
Group	653	518	137	243	224	19	296	274	22
Total	750	786	− 36	279	292	−13	335	354	−10

TABLE 24—*Continued*

	1928			1935			1938		
	X	M	B	X	M	B	X	M	B
			Finland						
Austria	0	1	− 1	0	1	− 1	0	2	− 2
Belgium–Lux.*	20	13	7	8	5	3	6	10	− 4
Czechoslovakia*	0	5	− 5	0	2	− 2	0	4	− 4
France*	19	9	10	6	3	3	6	4	2
Germany*	42	127	− 85	13	24	− 11	27	37	− 10
Italy	2	2	0	2	1	2	4	2	2
Netherlands*	22	16	6	4	4	0	8	8	0
Sweden*	6	28	− 22	7	13	− 6	9	24	− 15
Switzerland*	0	2	− 2	0	2	− 2	0	3	− 3
Bulgaria*	0	0	0	0	0	0	0	0	0
Denmark*	6	14	− 8	5	5	0	6	9	− 3
Estonia	2	5	− 3	1	3	− 2	1	2	− 1
Finland*	—	—	—	—	—	—	—	—	—
Greece	0	0	0	0	0	0	1	1	0
Hungary*	0	0	0	0	0	0	0	1	− 1
Norway	1	2	− 1	2	2	0	2	3	− 1
Poland	1	5	− 4	0	3	− 3	1	5	− 4
Portugal	0	0	0	0	0	0	0	0	0
Roumania	0	0	0	0	0	0	0	0	0
Spain	6	1	5	1	1	0	0	0	0
Turkey	0	0	0	1	0	1	1	0	1
Yugoslavia	0	0	0	0	0	0	0	0	0
United Kingdom*	94	43	51	64	28	36	81	38	43
Rest of World	34	64	− 30	19	15	4	26	28	− 2
Europe	222	273	− 51	115	97	18	154	153	1
Group	209	257	− 48	107	86	21	143	138	5
Total	267	342	− 75	136	116	20	181	183	− 2

TABLE 24—*Continued*

	1928			1935			1938		
	X	M	B	X	M	B	X	M	B
				Hungary					
Austria	83	58	25	25	22	3	28	14	14
Belgium–Lux.*	2	3	− 1	1	1	0	1	1	0
Czechoslovakia*	43	80	−37	6	6	0	6	8	− 2
France*	2	9	− 7	3	2	1	3	2	1
Germany*	29	70	−41	33	27	6	44	37	7
Italy	16	14	2	18	9	9	14	8	6
Netherlands*	1	7	− 6	1	3	− 2	2	4	− 2
Sweden*	1	1	0	1	0	1	3	1	2
Switzerland*	9	14	− 5	6	4	2	5	3	2
Bulgaria*	2	3	− 1	1	1	0	2	1	1
Denmark*	1	0	1	1	0	1	2	1	1
Estonia	0	0	0	0	0	0	0	0	0
Finland*	0	0	0	0	0	0	0	0	0
Greece	2	2	0	1	0	1	1	1	0
Hungary*	—	—	—	—	—	—	—	—	—
Norway	0	0	0	1	0	1	1	0	1
Poland	8	15	− 7	1	1	0	2	2	0
Portugal	0	0	0	0	0	0	0	0	0
Roumania	13	28	−15	7	16	− 9	6	12	− 6
Spain	1	1	0	1	0	1	0	0	0
Turkey	2	2	0	1	0	1	1	1	0
Yugoslavia	16	18	− 2	3	7	− 4	5	6	− 1
United Kingdom*	7	10	− 3	11	6	5	12	8	4
Rest of World	5	22	−17	10	12	− 2	17	12	5
Europe	238	335	−97	122	105	17	138	110	28
Group	97	197	−100	64	50	14	80	66	14
Total	244	358	−114	133	118	15	155	122	33

TABLE 24—*Continued*

	1928			1935			1938		
	X	M	B	X	M	B	X	M	B
	United Kingdom								
Austria	22	18	− 4	6	8	− 2	6	8	− 2
Belgium–Lux.*	140	354	−214	43	77	−34	40	93	−53
Czechoslovakia*	118	64	54	7	·21	−14	11	33	−22
France*	207	468	−261	82	101	−19	74	109	−35
Germany*	338	506	−168	94	143	−49	101	141	−40
Italy	119	121	− 2	33	36	− 3	28	33	− 5
Netherlands*	180	346	−166	58	109	−51	64	141	−77
Sweden*	80	179	−99	48	83	−35	57	119	−62
Switzerland*	65	108	−43	20	25	− 5	17	34	−17
Bulgaria*	7	1	6	1	2	− 1	1	2	− 1
Denmark*	80	434	−354	67	156	−89	76	185	−109
Estonia	18	67	−49	17	34	−17	23	47	−24
Finland*	30	108	−78	21	73	−52	27	93	−66
Greece	41	26	15	15	10	5	18	9	9
Hungary*	8	4	4	2	9	− 7	3	11	− 8
Norway	65	94	−29	32	39	− 7	35	51	−13
Poland	43	47	− 4	19	35	−16	26	46	−20
Portugal	33	28	5	22	16	6	16	18	− 2
Roumania	25	14	11	6	15	− 9	6	18	−12
Spain	81	143	−62	26	52	−26	17	25	− 8
Turkey	22	19	3	5	4	1	12	4	8
Yugoslavia	11	5	6	4	6	− 2	6	11	− 5
United Kingdom*	—	—	—	—	—	—	—	—	—
Rest of World	3968	5148	−1180	1314	2182	−868	1464	2740	−1276
Europe	1944	3525	−1581	742	1147	−405	781	1343	−562
Group	1253	2572	−1323	443	799	−356	471	961	−490
Total	5934	8821	−2887	2073	3426	−1353	2277	4161	−1884

TABLE 25
GROUP COUNTRIES PERCENTAGE CHANGE IN B

	Belgium–Lux.		Czechoslovakia	
	(1)	(2)	(1)	(2)
Belgium–Lux.	—	—	100.00	0
Czechoslovakia	− 3*	33.33	—	—
France	105.47	−128.57	88.88	− 33.33
Germany	−281.82	105.00	85.06	130.77
Netherlands	− 68.42	64.71	−100.00	+ 6*
Sweden	200.00	33.33	0	−200.00
Switzerland	− 59.09	11.11	− 57.14	− 33.33
Bulgaria	− 50.00	0	− 80.00	−200.00
Denmark	− 92.86	+100.00	− 91.67	0
Finland	64.71	83.33	− 60.00	50.00
Hungary	− 1*	100.00	−100.00	+ 3*
United Kingdom	− 66.22	15.63	− 78.13	128.57
Rest of World	5.00	− 46.05	130.77	−225.00
Europe	12.12	121.62	− 79.09	165.22
Group	314.29	131.03	100.00	+ 28*
Total	+ 3.64	+ 22.64	− 72.28	121.43

NOTE: (1) 1928–35, (2) 1935–38
*Percentage across a change in sign

	France		Germany	
	(1)	(2)	(1)	(2)
Belgium–Lux.	− 64.37	− 67.74	400.00	− 53.33
Czechoslovakia	100.00	+ 3*	− 88.64	0
France	—	—	153.23	− 9.09
Germany	−212.20	19.57	—	—
Netherlands	83.33	200.00	− 85.69	19.05
Sweden	70.83	28.57	− 70.83	− 95.24
Switzerland	− 76.97	− 25.71	− 40.82	− 29.31
Bulgaria	−150.00	200.00	83.33	−1000.00
Denmark	− 57.14	− 66.67	− 65.38	55.55
Finland	62.50	33.30	− 91.43	−200.00
Hungary	−200.00	−100.00	−118.00	−100.00
United Kingdom	− 98.84	400.00	− 58.62	− 43.75
Rest of World	49.44	− 30.77	89.52	−101.69
Europe	− 98.45	200.00	− 51.60	− 12.61
Group	− 98.96	366.66	− 70.28	− 23.40
Total	−286.32	− 21.53	106.38	−215.38

TABLE 25—*Continued*

	Netherlands		Sweden	
	(1)	(2)	(1)	(2)
Belgium–Lux.	75.58	− 42.86	−100.00	−300.00
Czechoslovakia	16.67	− 80.00	0	50.00
France	+ 2*	−250.00	− 85.71	−450.00
Germany	58.15	− 5.19	71.52	9.30
Netherlands	—	—	−100.00	− 33.33
Sweden	150.00	− 25.00	—	—
Switzerland	400.00	−100.00	20.00	−100.00
Bulgaria	− 1*	100.00	0	0
Denmark	−100.00	− 2*	0	− 16.67
Finland	90.91	−300.00	− 72.72	183.33
Hungary	−200.00	− 1*	− 1*	−200.00
United Kingdom	− 68.38	78.38	− 83.33	88.88
Rest of World	65.61	73.75	121.21	−500.00
Europe	63.97	− 28.57	− 37.84	35.29
Group	64.15	− 7.02	33.33	− 12.00
Total	64.24	− 50.28	− 25.00	33.33

	Switzerland		Bulgaria	
	(1)	(2)	(1)	(2)
Belgium–Lux.	70.59	− 20.00	0	+ 1*
Czechoslovakia	57.14	50.00	185.71	0
France	74.07	17.86	200.00	− 1*
Germany	31.25	32.73	150.00	−100.00
Netherlands	−500.00	120.00	−100.00	0
Sweden	− 80.00	500.00	200.00	−200.00
Switzerland	—	—	0	−100.00
Bulgaria	200.00	−100.00	—	—
Denmark	50.00	200.00	+ 1*	100.00
Finland	−200.00	+ 3*	0	0
Hungary	− 1*	−200.00	0	− 1*
United Kingdom	− 37.04	− 58.82	100.00	− 1*
Rest of World	− 15.38	90.00	300.00	− 50.00
Europe	21.19	53.78	111.11	600.00
Group	38.15	51.02	92.86	600.00
Total	14.69	58.94	130.00	166.66

TABLE 25—*Continued*

	Denmark		Finland	
	(1)	(2)	(1)	(2)
Belgium–Lux.	88.88	− 50.00	− 57.14	−233.33
Czechoslovakia	100.00	− 1*	60.00	−100.00
France	79.17	120.00	− 70.00	− 33.33
Germany	80.39	− 5.00	87.06	9.09
Netherlands	76.92	− 33.33	−100.00	0
Sweden	−100.00	−200.00	72.72	−150.00
Switzerland	−100.00	− 1*	0	− 50.00
Bulgaria	− 1*	0	0	0
Denmark	—	—	100.00	− 3*
Finland	−116.67	−100.00	—	—
Hungary	0	− 1*	0	− 1*
United Kingdom	−81.76	16.07	− 29.41	19.44
Rest of World	84.63	− 15.63	113.33	−150.00
Europe	−86.84	− 10.00	135.29	− 94.44
Group	− 86.13	15.79	143.75	76.19
Total	63.89	46.15	126.67	−110.00

	Hungary		United Kingdom	
	(1)	(2)	(1)	(2)
Belgium–Lux.	100.00	0	84.11	− 55.88
Czechoslovakia	+100.00	− 2*	−125.93	− 36.36
France	114.29	0	92.72	− 84.21
Germany	114.63	16.67	70.83	22.50
Netherlands	66.67	0	69.28	− 50.98
Sweden	+ 1*	100.00	64.64	− 77.14
Switzerland	140.00	0	88.37	− 70.59
Bulgaria	100.00	+ 1*	−112.50	0
Denmark	0	0	74.86	− 22.47
Finland	0	0	33.33	− 26.92
Hungary	—	—	−275.00	− 14.29
United Kingdom	266.67	− 20.00	—	—
Rest of World	88.24	350.00	26.44	− 47.00
Europe	114.00	64.71	74.38	− 38.77
Group	153.85	0	71.75	− 37.64
Total	113.16	120.00	53.13	39.25

TABLE 26
PERCENTAGE CHANGE IN X, M

	Belgium–Luxemburg			
	X		M	
	(1)	(2)	(1)	(2)
Belgium–Lux.	—	—	—	—
Czechoslovakia	− 50.00	+100.00	0	+ 33.33
France	− 44.74	+ 4.76	− 69.18	+ 14.29
Germany	− 70.89	+ 55.17	− 58.51	+ 14.10
Netherlands	− 66.47	+ 35.38	− 67.04	+ 20.03
Sweden	0	+ 66.67	− 40.00	+ 77.78
Switzerland	− 55.56	+ 18.75	− 50.00	+ 28.57
Bulgaria	− 66.67	0	−100.00	+ 1*
Denmark	− 66.67	+ 20.00	+300.00	0
Finland	− 50.00	+ 75.00	− 60.00	− 20.00
Hungary	−100.00	+ 1*	0	0
United Kingdom	− 68.09	+ 19.51	− 70.59	+ 22.00
Group	− 61.89	+ 27.07	− 64.77	+ 17.70
Europe	− 60.62	+ 25.12	− 63.63	+ 15.45
Rest of World	− 61.96	+ 26.42	− 52.81	+ 32.77
Total	− 60.56	+ 26.57	− 58.50	+ 22.40

NOTE: (1) 1928–35, (2) 1935–38
*Percentage across a change in sign

	Czechoslovakia			
	X		M	
	(1)	(2)	(1)	(2)
Belgium–Lux.	− 12.50	0	− 53.33	0
Czechoslovakia	—	—	—	—
France	− 7.14	− 30.77	− 60.98	− 18.75
Germany	− 82.39	+ 18.00	− 83.02	− 12.70
Netherlands	− 36.74	+ 25.00	− 14.29	− 25.00
Sweden	− 46.67	+ 25.00	− 53.85	+100.00
Switzerland	− 64.52	+ 9.09	− 66.67	+ 25.00
Bulgaria	− 55.56	− 50.00	− 25.00	0
Denmark	− 78.57	− 33.33	0	− 50.00
Finland	− 60.00	+100.00	0	+ 1*
Hungary	− 91.89	+ 50.00	− 86.05	0
United Kingdom	− 68.92	+ 39.13	− 61.90	0
Group	− 74.59	+ 15.83	− 57.57	− 4.51
Europe	− 74.12	+ 10.59	− 73.44	− 6.10
Rest of World	− 48.89	+ 21.74	− 56.08	+ 36.92
Total	− 70.88	+ 14.56	− 70.73	+ 3.91

TABLE 26—*Continued*

	France X		M	
	(1)	(2)	(1)	(2)
Belgium–Lux.	− 77.13	− 0.83	− 65.30	− 3.33
Czechoslovakia	0	− 7.69	− 7.14	− 30.77
France	—	—	—	—
Germany	− 81.23	− 24.29	− 65.06	− 22.41
Netherlands	− 75.28	+ 22.58	− 69.03	− 2.86
Sweden	− 36.84	+ 16.67	− 55.81	0
Switzerland	− 67.76	− 20.29	− 45.16	− 14.71
Bulgaria	− 100.00	+ 2*	− 50.00	0
Denmark	− 55.00	− 44.44	− 50.00	0
Finland	− 57.14	+ 33.33	− 60.87	− 11.11
Hungary	− 66.67	0	0	+ 50.00
United Kingdom	− 79.58	− 4.67	− 70.17	− 12.38
Group	− 75.71	− 6.88	− 64.67	− 12.09
Europe	− 75.48	− 10.56	− 65.58	− 14.53
Rest of World	− 61.87	− 18.18	− 57.31	+ 3.10
Total	− 70.31	− 14.62	− 60.77	− 5.10

	Germany X		M	
	(1)	(2)	(1)	(2)
Belgium–Lux.	− 58.88	+ 13.58	− 73.30	+ 52.94
Czechoslovakia	− 80.08	+ 5.77	− 77.42	+ 6.12
France	− 67.69	− 19.32	− 81.40	− 19.44
Germany	—	—	—	—
Netherlands	− 81.35	+ 10.43	− 72.48	+ 1.27
Sweden	− 52.30	+ 28.92	− 39.22	+ 70.97
Switzerland	− 54.98	− 20.19	− 65.41	− 8.70
Bulgaria	+ 6.67	+ 43.75	− 19.05	+ 100.00
Denmark	− 66.07	+ 42.11	− 66.20	+ 39.58
Finland	− 76.74	+ 65.00	− 66.67	+ 111.76
Hungary	− 46.77	+ 76.00	+ 6.90	+ 41.94
United Kingdom	− 68.28	− 7.28	− 71.39	+ 9.71
Group	− 70.13	+ 8.05	− 70.05	+ 23.48
Europe	− 64.44	+ 21.69	− 65.84	+ 27.41
Rest of World	− 61.35	+ 38.23	− 77.87	+ 55.85
Total	− 64.54	+ 25.77	− 70.56	+ 33.29

TABLE 26—*Continued*

	Netherlands			
	X		M	
	(1)	(2)	(1)	(2)
Belgium–Lux.	− 58.82	+ 18.37	− 65.85	+ 25.71
Czechoslovakia	− 30.00	0	− 25.00	+ 33.33
France	− 60.98	+ 3.13	− 63.41	+ 20.00
Germany	− 72.29	− 3.45	− 67.07	+ 0.61
Netherlands	—	—	—	—
Sweden	− 35.00	+ 50.00	− 64.29	+ 70.00
Switzerland	− 41.67	0	− 56.25	+ 71.43
Bulgaria	−100.00	0	0	−100.00
Denmark	− 85.71	+ 33.33	− 40.00	+100.00
Finland	− 72.73	+ 66.67	− 81.82	+120.00
Hungary	− 66.67	0	0	+100.00
United Kingdom	− 66.78	+ 32.99	− 65.71	+ 5.00
Group	− 65.73	+ 15.74	− 65.49	+ 14.36
Europe	− 64.69	+ 13.07	− 64.61	+ 15.21
Rest of World	− 70.09	+ 58.59	− 67.80	− 13.76
Total	− 65.59	+ 24.02	− 65.22	+ 21.89

	Sweden			
	X		M	
	(1)	(2)	(1)	(2)
Belgium–Lux.	− 41.18	+ 40.00	− 33.33	+ 83.33
Czechoslovakia	− 57.14	+200.00	− 44.44	+ 57.14
France	− 65.85	− 64.29	− 55.56	+ 33.33
Germany	− 46.67	+ 70.83	− 62.24	+ 32.97
Netherlands	− 68.75	+ 70.00	− 38.71	+ 52.63
Sweden	—	—	—	—
Switzerland	− 33.33	+ 50.00	− 25.00	+ 83.33
Bulgaria	0	0	0	0
Denmark	− 58.70	+ 15.79	− 51.92	+ 16.00
Finland	− 59.26	+100.00	0	0
Hungary	−100.00	+ 1*	0	+300.00
United Kingdom	− 54.19	+ 37.80	− 41.60	+ 31.51
Group	− 54.98	+ 44.72	− 51.64	+ 37.05
Europe	− 54.95	+ 98.78	− 49.06	+ 34.34
Rest of World	− 47.74	+ 14.81	− 60.64	+ 63.51
Total	− 53.85	+ 40.30	− 51.61	+ 39.47

TABLE 26—*Continued*

| | Switzerland | | | |
| | X | | M | |
	(1)	(2)	(1)	(2)
Belgium–Lux.	− 50.00	+ 42.85	− 61.29	+ 33.33
Czechoslovakia	− 58.82	+ 42.85	− 58.06	0
France	− 37.25	− 12.50	− 62.26	− 15.00
Germany	− 55.28	− 18.96	− 45.81	+ 52.72
Netherlands	− 55.55	+ 75.00	− 29.41	+ 8.33
Sweden	− 44.44	+ 80.00	0	0
Switzerland	—	—	—	—
Bulgaria	+100.00	− 50.00	− 50.00	0
Denmark	− 50.00	+ 33.33	− 50.00	− 25.00
Finland	− 50.00	+200.00	+ 1*	−100.00
Hungary	− 33.33	− 25.00	− 16.67	+ 20.00
United Kingdom	− 75.00	+ 36.00	− 45.65	− 20.00
Group	− 57.06	+ 9.40	− 5.28	− 14.57
Europe	− 57.59	+ 4.41	− 48.89	− 17.03
Rest of World	− 73.91	+ 57.41	− 63.95	+ 4.76
Total	− 62.46	+ 16.22	− 52.71	− 11.46

| | Bulgaria | | | |
| | X | | M | |
	(1)	(2)	(1)	(2)
Belgium–Lux.	−100.00	+ 1*	−100.00	0
Czechoslovakia	+ 50.00	0	− 55.56	0
France	− 80.00	0	− 85.71	+100.00
Germany	− 9.52	+ 84.21	+ 11.11	+ 40.00
Netherlands	− 66.67	0	− 50.00	0
Sweden	+ 1*	−100.00	−100.00	+ 1*
Switzerland	0	0	0	− 50.00
Bulgaria	—	—	—	—
Denmark	+ 1*	+100.00	0	0
Finland	0	0	0	0
Hungary	− 50.00	0	− 50.00	+100.00
United Kingdom	0	+ 50.00	− 77.78	+100.00
Group	− 23.08	+ 56.67	− 41.51	+ 35.48
Europe	− 50.00	+ 72.97	− 56.63	+ 58.33
Rest of World	+ 50.00	+ 33.33	− 66.67	+200.00
Total	− 43.37	+ 70.00	− 56.98	+ 62.16

TABLE 26—*Continued*

	Denmark			
	X		M	
	(1)	(2)	(1)	(2)
Belgium–Lux.	+ 100.00	+ 25.00	− 70.00	+ 33.33
Czechoslovakia	+ 100.00	− 50.00	− 75.00	0
France	− 40.00	+ 66.67	− 72.91	− 50.00
Germany	− 70.97	+ 46.67	− 74.71	+ 33.85
Netherlands	− 50.00	+ 100.00	− 71.88	+ 55.56
Sweden	− 63.27	− 5.56	− 60.00	+ 15.00
Switzerland	− 62.50	0	− 50.00	+ 33.33
Bulgaria	0	0	+ 1*	0
Denmark	—	—	—	—
Finland	− 69.23	+ 25.00	− 28.57	+ 40.00
Hungary	0	0	0	+ 1*
United Kingdom	− 61.30	+ 16.77	− 3.67	+ 17.14
Group	− 62.79	+ 21.81	− 56.76	+ 22.32
Europe	− 63.51	+ 17.91	− 56.18	+ 20.16
Rest of World	− 63.33	+ 72.73	− 81.73	+ 34.21
Total	− 62.80	+ 20.07	− 62.85	+ 21.23

	Finland			
	X		M	
	(1)	(2)	(1)	(2)
Belgium–Lux.	− 60.00	− 25.00	− 61.54	+ 100.00
Czechoslovakia	0	0	− 60.00	+ 100.00
France	− 68.42	0	− 66.67	+ 33.33
Germany	− 69.05	+ 107.69	− 81.10	+ 54.17
Netherlands	− 81.82	+ 100.00	− 75.00	+ 100.00
Sweden	+ 16.67	+ 28.57	− 53.57	+ 84.62
Switzerland	0	0	0	+ 50.00
Bulgaria	0	0	0	0
Denmark	− 16.67	+ 20.00	− 64.29	+ 80.00
Finland	—	—	—	—
Hungary	0	0	0	+ 1*
United Kingdom	− 31.91	+ 26.56	− 34.88	+ 35.71
Group	− 48.80	+ 33.64	− 66.54	+ 60.47
Europe	− 48.20	+ 33.91	− 64.47	+ 57.73
Rest of World	− 44.12	+ 36.84	− 76.56	+ 86.67
Total	− 49.06	+ 33.09	− 66.08	+ 57.76

TABLE 26—*Continued*

	Hungary			
	X		M	
	(1)	(2)	(1)	(2)
Belgium–Lux.	− 50.00	0	− 66.67	0
Czechoslovakia	− 86.05	0	− 92.50	+ 33.33
France	+ 50.00	0	− 77.76	0
Germany	+ 13.79	+ 33.33	− 61.43	+ 37.04
Netherlands	0	+100.00	− 57.14	+ 33.33
Sweden	0	+200.00	−100.00	+ 1*
Switzerland	− 33.33	− 16.67	− 71.43	− 25.00
Bulgaria	− 50.00	+100.00	− 66.67	0
Denmark	0	+100.00	0	+ 1*
Finland	0	0	0	0
Hungary	—	—	—	—
United Kingdom	+ 57.14	+ 9.09	− 40.00	+ 33.30
Group	− 34.02	+ 25.00	− 74.62	+ 32.00
Europe	− 48.74	+ 13.11	− 68.66	+ 4.76
Rest of World	+100.00	+ 70.00	− 45.45	0
Total	− 45.49	+ 16.54	− 67.04	+ 3.39

	United Kingdom			
	X		M	
	(1)	(2)	(1)	(2)
Belgium–Lux.	− 69.28	− 6.97	− 78.24	+ 20.77
Czechoslovakia	− 94.06	+ 57.14	− 67.18	+ 57.14
France	− 69.29	− 9.75	− 78.41	+ 7.92
Germany	− 72.18	+ 7.44	− 71.73	− 1.40
Netherlands	− 67.77	+ 10.34	− 68.49	+ 29.35
Sweden	− 40.00	+ 18.75	− 53.63	+ 43.37
Switzerland	− 69.23	− 15.00	− 76.85	+ 36.00
Bulgaria	− 85.71	0	+100.00	0
Denmark	− 16.25	+ 13.43	− 64.05	+ 18.58
Finland	− 30.00	+ 28.57	− 32.40	+ 27.40
Hungary	− 75.00	+ 50.00	+125.00	+ 22.22
United Kingdom	—	—	—	—
Group	− 64.64	+ 6.32	− 68.93	− 20.28
Europe	− 61.83	+ 5.25	− 67.46	+ 17.08
Rest of World	− 66.88	+ 11.41	− 57.61	+ 25.57
Total	− 65.06	+ 9.84	− 61.16	+ 21.45

References

(1) Ashley, P. *Modern tariff policy, Germany–United States–France*. London, 1920.

(2) Barnes, D. G. *A history of the English Corn Laws*. New York: F. S. Crofts, 1930.

(3) Benham, F. *Great Britain under protection*. New York: Macmillan, 1941.

(4) Beveridge, W. H., et al. *Tariffs, the case examined*. London, New York, Toronto: Longman, Green, 1931.

(5) Bhagwati, J. *Trade, tariffs and growth*. Cambridge: MIT Press, 1969.

(6) Bhagwati, J., ed. *International trade*. Middlesex, England: Penguin Books, 1969.

(7) Bhagwati, J., and Ramaswani, V. K. Domestic distortions tariffs, and the theory of optimum subsidy. *Journal of Political Economy* (February 1963).

(8) Chalmers, H. *World trade policies*. Berkeley and Los Angeles: University of California Press, 1953.

(9) Chang, T. C. *Cyclical movements in the balance of payments*. Cambridge: At the University Press, 1951.

(10) Cheng, H. S. *Statistical estimates of elasticities and propensities in international trade: a survey of published studies*. IMF Staff Papers, vols. 6–7, pp. 107–58. 1960.

(11) Chow, G. C. Tests of equality between subsets of coefficients in two linear regressions. *Econometrica* (1960).

(12) Condliffe, J. B. *The reconstruction of world trade, a survey of international economic relations*. New York: W. W. Norton, 1940.

(13) Corbo, V. Private consumption in England 1860–1950. Manuscript, MIT, 1970.

(14) Friedman, P. On the theory and measurement of bilateralism. Working paper 73–09, University of Florida.

(15) Hall, R. Econometric notes. Mimeo, MIT, 1970.

(16) Heuser, H. *Control of international trade*. Philadelphia: P. Blakiston's Son & Co., 1939.

(17) Hodson, H. V. *Slump and recovery 1929–1937, a survey of world economic affairs*. London, New York, Toronto: Oxford University Press, 1938.

(18) Isaacs, A. *International trade, tariff and commercial policies*. Chicago: Richard D. Irwin, Inc., 1948.

(19) Johnson, H. The transfer problem and exchange stability. *Journal of Political Economy* (June 1956).

(20) Johnson, H. Economic expansion and international trade. *Manchester School of Economic Social Studies* (May 1955).

(21) Johnston, J. *Econometric methods.* New York: McGraw-Hill, 1963.
(22) Jones, Joseph M., Jr. *Tariff retaliation.* Philadelphia: University of Pennsylvania Press, 1934.
(23) Keynes, John Maynard. *The economic consequences of the peace.* New York: Harcourt, Brace and Howe, Inc., 1920.
(24) Kindleberger, C. P. *International economics.* Homewood, Ill.: Richard D. Irwin, 1963.
(25) Kindleberger, C. P. *The world in depression, 1929–1939.* London: Allan Lane, 1972.
(26) Leamer, Edward E., and Stern, Robert M. *Quantitative international economics.* Boston: Allyn & Bacon, 1970.
(27) Lewis, W. A. *Economic survey 1919–1939.* Philadelphia: Blakiston, 1950.
(28) Liepmann, H. *Tariff levels and the economic unity of Europe.* London: George Allen & Unwin Ltd., 1938.
(29) Mundell, R. A. *International economics.* New York: Macmillan, 1968.
(30) Neisser, H., and Modigliani, F. *National incomes and international trade, a quantitative analysis.* Urbana: University of Illinois Press, 1953.
(31) Nurkse, R. *International currency experience.* New York: Columbia University Press, 1944.
(32) Polak, J. J. *An international economic system.* London: George Allen & Unwin Ltd., 1954.
(33) Snyder, R. C. *The most-favored-nation clause.* New York: Columbia University, 1948.
(34) Woytinsky, W. S., and Woytinsky, E. S. *World commerce and governments.* New York: Twentieth Century Fund, 1955.
(35) American Economic Association. *Readings in the theory of international trade.* Homewood, Ill.: Richard D. Irwin, 1950.
(36) American Economic Association. *Readings in international economics.* Homewood, Ill.: Richard D. Irwin, 1968.
(37) League of Nations. *Balance of payments.* Geneva, 1930–45.
(38) League of Nations. *Commercial policy in the interwar period: international proposals and national policies.* Geneva, 1942.
(39) League of Nations. *International trade statistics.* Geneva, 1937.
(40) League of Nations. *Europe's trade.* Geneva, 1941.
(41) League of Nations. *Monthly bulletin of statistics.* Geneva, January 1928–December 1939.
(42) United Nations. *National income statistics.* New York: Statistical Office of the United Nations, 1950.
(43) League of Nations. *Network of world trade.* Geneva, 1942.
(44) League of Nations. *Review of world trade 1936–1938.* Geneva, 1939.
(45) League of Nations. *International economic commission report.* Geneva, 1927.
(46) U.S. Department of Commerce. *The United States in the world economy.* Washington, 1943.
(47) League of Nations. *World economic survey 1931–1939.* 8 vols. Geneva, 1940.

UNIVERSITY OF FLORIDA MONOGRAPHS

Social Sciences

24. *Aymara Communities and the Bolivian Agrarian Reform*, by William E. Carter

25. *Conservatives in the Progressive Era: The Taft Republicans of 1912*, by Norman M. Wilensky

26. *The Anglo-Norwegian Fisheries Case of 1951 and the Changing Law of the Territorial Sea*, by Teruo Kobayashi

27. *The Liquidity Structure of Firms and Monetary Economics*, by William J. Frazer, Jr.

28. *Russo-Persian Commercial Relations, 1828–1914*, by Marvin L. Entner

29. *The Imperial Policy of Sir Robert Borden*, by Harold A. Wilson

30. *The Association of Income and Educational Achievement*, by Roy L. Lassiter, Jr.

31. *Relation of the People to the Land in Southern Iraq*, by Fuad Baali

32. *The Price Theory of Value in Public Finance*, by Donald R. Escarraz

33. *The Process of Rural Development in Latin America*, by T. Lynn Smith

34. *To Be or Not to Be . . . Existential-Psychological Perspectives on the Self*, edited by Sidney M. Jourard

35. *Politics in a Mexican Community*, by Lawrence S. Graham

36. *A Two-Sector Model of Economic Growth with Technological Progress*, by Frederick Owen Goddard

37. *Florida Studies in the Helping Professions*, by Arthur W. Combs

38. *The Ancient Synagogues of the Iberian Peninsula*, by Don A. Halperin

39. *An Estimate of Personal Wealth in Oklahoma in 1960*, by Richard Edward French

40. *Congressional Oversight of Executive Agencies*, by Thomas A. Henderson

41. *Historians and Meiji Statesmen*, by Richard T. Chang

42. *Welfare Economics and Peak Load Pricing: A Theoretical Application to Municipal Water Utility Practices*, by Robert Lee Greene

43. *Factor Analysis in International Relations: Interpretation, Problem Areas, and an Application*, by Jack E. Vincent

44. *The Sorcerer's Apprentice: The French Scientist's Image of German Science, 1840–1919*, by Harry W. Paul

45. *Community Power Structure: Propositional Inventory, Tests, and Theory*, by Claire W. Gilbert

46. *Human Capital, Technology, and the Role of the United States in International Trade*, by John F. Morrall III

47. *The Segregation Factor in the Florida Democratic Gubernatorial Primary of 1956*, by Helen L. Jacobstein

48. *The Navy Department in the War of 1812*, by Edward K. Eckert

49. *Social Change and the Electoral Process*, by William L. Shade

50. *East from the Andes: Pioneer Settlements in the South American Heartland*, by Raymond E. Crist and Charles M. Nissly

51. *A General Equilibrium Study of the Monetary Mechanism*, by David L. Schulze

52. *The Impact of Trade Destruction on National Incomes: A Study of Europe 1924–1938*, by Philip Friedman